Aid,
Influence,
and
Foreign Policy

Aid,
Influence,
and
Foreign Policy

Joan M. Nelson
The Center for International Affairs
HARVARD UNIVERSITY

The Macmillan Company, New York
Collier-Macmillan Limited, London

First Printing

Written under the Auspices of
The Center for International Affairs
Harvard University

Library of Congress catalog card number: 68–10383

THE MACMILLAN COMPANY, NEW YORK
COLLIER-MACMILLAN CANADA, LTD., TORONTO, ONTARIO

PRINTED IN THE UNITED STATES OF AMERICA

To P. C.

Acknowledgments

This book is only in part my own. To a large degree, I have written it as the rapporteur of ideas developed from 1962 to 1966 by past and present members of the Program Coordination Staff of the Agency for International Development. In particular, the chapters on allocation criteria and types of country programs, on program planning, and on the use of aid to influence development policies owe a great deal to Hollis Chenery, Gustav Ranis, Lester Gordon, Bartlett Harvey, Clarence Gulick, Alan Strout, David Cole, and Karl Mathiasen. Much of the discussion of aid and long-run political development was originally worked out with Eugene Mihaly. The work on short-run political uses of aid is my own.

For helpful suggestions on the book itself I am indebted to my editor, Paul Hammond, to Robert J. Patterson, Political Science Editor for The Macmillan Company, and to Robert Erwin, Editor of Publications for The Center for International Affairs of Harvard University. Particular thanks for thoughtful and constructive criticism go to my father, Saul Nelson, and to Margot and Bartlett Harvey, Hollis Chenery, Karl Mathiasen, and David Cole. Lester Gordon, Samuel Huntington, David Britt, Paula Tosini, and John Schott also gave me valuable suggestions on all or parts of the manuscript. I would also like to express my appreciation to The Center for International Affairs of Harvard University for its support, and to Jane Tatlock for her typing assistance.

Needless to say, despite the group origin of many of the concepts in the book, I remain entirely responsible for the statement of those concepts and for the judgments expressed.

J. M. N.

Contents

Introduction

FOREIGN AID has become a major instrument of U.S. foreign policy throughout the underdeveloped world. In many countries, it is the primary instrument relied upon to protect and promote central U.S. interests. As a result, the economic assistance program has come to serve and to reflect the full range of U.S. interests in the developing countries. These interests are as humanitarian as relieving poverty and disease; as manipulative as attempting to influence the outcome of an election; as ephemeral as concern over the tenor of remarks of tomorrow's U.N. General Assembly session; as long-run as investment in a country's capacity to maintain growth without external aid. This multipurpose nature of aid is a major cause of uncertainty about its goals and its effectiveness. Senator J. W. Fulbright (Democrat, Arkansas), Chairman of the Senate Foreign Relations Committee and for many years the manager of the annual foreign assistance bills in the Senate, has stated:

> It is a misnomer to speak of *the* foreign aid program. It is not *a* program; it is a conglomeration of programs—to support foreign armies; to maintain American military bases in foreign lands; to build roads, dams, steel mills; to pay foreigners' import bills; to grow more food; to rent communication stations; to train foreign tax collectors; to provide emergency relief from natural disasters; and to support multifarious United Nations activities which themselves range from feeding children, to killing malarial mosquitoes, to irrigating Pakistan.
>
> Quite clearly there is nothing inherently wrong about any of these purposes. . . . [But] it is no wonder that the Congress, the public, and perhaps the Administration has difficulty in understanding the [assistance effort].[1]

This book does not attempt to examine thoroughly the full range of foreign assistance goals and aid's effectiveness in serving them, nor to explore systematically the conflicts and complementarities among these goals. It has two more modest aims. Part I provides an introductory overview of the objectives the U.S. Government intends economic aid to promote, and the ways in which aid is employed to these ends. Like any instrument of foreign (or domestic)

---

[1] Senator J. W. Fulbright, "The Foreign Assistance Program," release dated March 4, 1965.

policy, aid often does not achieve its intended purposes, or does so only partially. Sometimes the unintended and unanticipated effects of aid may be adverse. But a clear picture of intended goals and means is a prerequisite to responsible assessment of results.

Part II explores more thoroughly the potential and limits of U.S. economic aid as an instrument for influencing aid-receiving countries' development policies, aspects of their current politics or foreign policies, and their long-run political evolution. Aid's role in supplementing scarce resources—human and financial—has been discussed extensively elsewhere.[2] Its role as influence has been less closely examined, and is more controversial. Yet much of aid's value as a flexible and multipurpose instrument of foreign policy springs from the ways in which it can be used to influence actions in other nations, rather than from its resource-transfer function.

The book focuses on that part of U.S. assistance administered by the Agency for International Development (A.I.D.). In recent years this has constituted roughly half of total U.S. economic aid. With the partial exception of the Food for Peace program, the criteria governing the administration of other elements of U.S. economic aid [3] are quite different from those that A.I.D. applies. Attempting to include them in the discussion would make an already complex topic unmanageable.

The Historical Background

Aid is a relatively new tool of U.S. foreign policy, although interstate subsidies are no innovation in the history of international relations.[4] Current U.S. aid programs have evolved from U.S. responses since World War II to successive problems and challenges.

[2] See, for example, Hollis B. Chenery and Alan M. Strout, "Foreign Assistance and Economic Development," *American Economic Review,* Vol. LVI, No. 4, September 1966, pp. 679–733; I. M. D. Little and J. M. Clifford, *International Aid,* Aldine Publishing Company, Chicago, 1966, Part II; Angus Maddison, *Foreign Skills and Technical Assistance in Economic Development,* Development Centre of the Organization for Economic Cooperation and Development, Paris, 1965.

[3] Other major elements of U.S. governmental aid include the Food for Peace program, administered jointly by the U.S. Department of Agriculture and A.I.D.; long-term loans from the Export-Import Bank; occasional U.S. Treasury loans, usually extended to assist financial stabilization; Peace Corps programs; and U.S. contributions to international organizations, including the various United Nations agencies, the World Bank and its soft-loan affiliate, the International Development Association, the Inter-American Development Bank and the Asian Development Bank.

[4] See George Liska, *The New Statecraft: Foreign Aid in American Foreign Policy,* University of Chicago Press, Chicago, 1960, Chapter II, for a discussion of the use of subsidies in Renaissance and post-Renaissance Europe.

The immediate and urgent need of the postwar period (1946–1948) was relief and rehabilitation. In that period the United States provided more than $11 billion to European nations for essential supplies such as food and fuel and for rehabilitation of damaged or destroyed facilities. But continued dislocation and the growing strength of the French, Italian, and Belgian Communist parties made it clear that relief was not enough: a massive reconstruction program was essential to preserve a free Western Europe. With the Marshall Plan the United States committed itself to provide the external financial support needed for recovery, while the European nations agreed to take both necessary domestic measures and steps toward European economic cooperation. Between mid-1948 and mid-1952, the United States financed more than $12 billion for European recovery. The results were spectacularly successful.

During the Korean War, the focus of Cold War concern swung from Europe to Asia, and emphasis shifted from recovery to containment and security. In the period from 1953 to 1957, the countries bordering on the Soviet Union and Communist China—Greece, Turkey, Iran, Pakistan, Thailand, Indochina (after partition, Cambodia, Laos and Vietnam), Taiwan, the Philippines, and Korea received the greatest part of U.S. economic aid, as well as extensive military aid.

Already, however, a third challenge was taking shape. In 1947, India and Pakistan won independence from colonial rule; Burma, Ceylon, Indonesia, and Indochina followed in the next few years; in 1951 Libya became the first of 36 African nations that have since become independent. Most of these nations were either in principle neutral, or leaned towards the West but were at bottom little concerned with the Cold War, which dominated the international scene. Their burning need and desire was development— economic and social progress to relieve appalling poverty and to convert nominal nationhood into the substance of economic and political self-reliance.

As early as 1949, President Truman had declared as "Point Four" of his inaugural address America's intention to make available to the new nations the knowledge and technology of the United States, by providing advisors to work abroad and offering training in the United States. Throughout the 1950's, emphasis on aid for economic and social progress grew. It became increasingly clear that development required not only "know-how," but also funds to buy the equipment and materials the developing countries needed but could not yet produce themselves. In 1958 the Development Loan Fund

(DLF) was established to finance development projects at lower interest rates and over longer repayment periods than commercial banks or the Export-Import Bank would provide.

Meanwhile, many Latin American countries made good progress in the early 1950's, benefiting from Korean War-inflated prices for their exports of minerals and foodstuffs. But prices fell in the wake of the truce, leaving disappointed hopes to feed unrest. By 1959 these pressures, linked with increasingly clear Communist control of the revolution in Cuba, confronted the United States with the prospect of widespread subversion of much of Latin America. Responding directly to this threat as well as to growing international emphasis on development, in 1960 the United States joined with the Latin American republics to sign the Act of Bogota. In March of the following year, President Kennedy called for an Alliance for Progress, and in August 1961 the Charter of Punta del Este laid down the principles for inter-American cooperation on a ten-year program for social and economic development.

Reflecting these events, U.S. economic aid to Latin America and Africa increased sharply. Assistance to the Far East dropped somewhat, while programs in South Asia, particularly India, expanded. Economic aid to European nations and Japan, already low by the mid-1950's, was entirely terminated.

Paralleling the geographic shift, the content of the aid program increasingly emphasized development. In the 1950's, military assistance and that part of economic aid which financed defense support or other security objectives were roughly double the level of developmental aid. In the 1960's, that ratio has been reversed.

These changes called for new legislation and new executive organization. In March 1961 President Kennedy's first message to Congress on foreign aid declared:

Existing foreign aid programs and concepts are largely unsatisfactory and unsuited for our needs and the needs of the underdeveloped world as it enters the sixties. . . . There exists, in the 1960s, a historic opportunity for a major economic assistance effort by the free industrialized nations to move more than half the people of the less-developed nations into self-sustained economic growth, while the rest move substantially closer to the day when they, too, will no longer have to depend on outside assistance. . . . To achieve this new goal we will need to renew the spirit of common effort which lay behind our past efforts—we must also revise our foreign aid organization, and our basic concepts of operation to meet the new problems which now confront us.[5]

[5] Excerpts from the Message of the President to Congress on foreign aid, transmitted on March 22, 1961.

Changing Geographic Allocation of U.S. Economic Aid, 1949–1966 (A.I.D. and Predecessor Agencies)

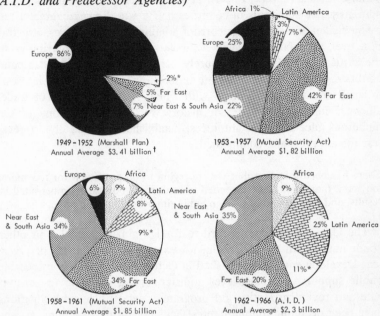

1949–1952 (Marshall Plan)
Annual Average $3.41 billion †

1953–1957 (Mutual Security Act)
Annual Average $1.82 billion

1958–1961 (Mutual Security Act)
Annual Average $1.85 billion

1962–1966 (A.I.D.)
Annual Average $2.3 billion

* Contributions to international organizations; administrative and other nonregional expenses.
† Period covers four-and-a-quarter years, from April 1948 through fiscal year 1952.

Source: A.I.D., *U.S. Overseas Loans and Grants, 1945–1965,* and *Operations Report,* FY 1966.

In response, Congress passed the Foreign Assistance Act of 1961 to replace the Mutual Security Act of 1954 as the fundamental guideline and authority for both military and economic aid programs. In the same year, the Agency for International Development was created to administer the economic aid program, combining the Development Loan Fund and the International Cooperation Administration (ICA), which had been responsible for technical assistance ("Point Four") and defense support.

In the five years following the establishment of A.I.D., many changes and improvements have been introduced into the economic assistance programs. A number of countries where the United States has a major commitment have made substantial progress; several can now maintain their further growth unaided. Yet after a brief reprise following the fresh start of 1961, Congressional and public doubts about the purpose and efficacy of foreign aid have reappeared as strong or stronger than before.

Some of the doubts may spring from disappointed expectations of rapid change—expectations that were unrealistic in the first instance. Some criticism reflects concern at inability to maintain normal U.S. administrative standards in countries half a world away characterized by inefficient and sometimes corrupt administrative practices. Frustration over aid's failure to win demonstrated gratitude contributes to the criticism. Uneasiness is surely also fed by more fundamental doubts regarding the appropriate nature and extent of U.S. interests in small and remote countries with which we have no ties of trade, alliance, cultural exchange, or historic relationship. As one of the numerous blue-ribbon committees, established periodically to reassess the aid program, commented:

There has been a feeling that we are trying to do too much for too many too soon, that we are overextended in resources and undercompensated in results, and that no end of foreign aid is either in sight or in mind.[6]

The U.S. malaise with regard to foreign aid is paralleled in other donor nations. In Great Britain, for example, the Ministry of Overseas Development was established in October 1964, with considerable public support, a cabinet-level minister, and a mandate to consolidate and revitalize British aid programs. Yet British aid obligations have been declining, public interest has cooled, and the ministry was recently dropped from cabinet status.

Yet objectively, foreign economic aid is a very small and declining burden on the United States, and is not a major burden in other advanced nations. In the Marshall Plan era, economic assistance claimed about 2 per cent of Gross National Product (GNP) and about 11 per cent of the Federal Budget; in 1966 it absorbed about 0.29 per cent of GNP and 1.9 per cent of the Budget.[7] Even if U.S. foreign assistance is more broadly construed to include not only A.I.D. expenditures but also military aid, contributions to international organizations, Food for Peace, and the Peace Corps, costs have dropped from a peak of 28 per cent of Federal expenditures in 1947 to 4.4 per cent in 1966. Although some other donors devote substantially more of their national income to foreign assistance than does the United States (France, for instance provides aid estimated at roughly 1 per cent of GNP), the total volume of free world economic aid commitments has remained roughly constant at

[6] Committee to Strengthen the Security of the Free World (Clay Committee), *Report to the President,* March 20, 1963, p. 1.

[7] A.I.D., *Summary Presentation to the Congress,* FY 1967, p. 18.

$6 billion for the last four years, while the U.S. share has also been relatively stable at about 60 per cent of the total.[8]

From the developing nations' standpoint, a constant total flow of aid represents a declining per capita flow. But needs are not declining. On the contrary, in a number of major nations disease control and public health measures have caused population growth to outpace increases in food production, raising the spectre of repeated and ever more serious famines. And capacity to use aid effectively is increasing. The governments of the developing nations are gradually building up a reservoir of skills and experience, which steadily improves their ability to plan and carry out development programs. Moreover, technological and economic research are constantly improving our knowledge of how to promote growth—although serious gaps remain. It is at least as true today as in 1961 that, in the words of President Kennedy, "We have not only obligations to fulfill, we have great opportunities to realize."

Forms of Economic Aid

For the reader not familiar with the economic assistance program, a brief glance at the forms of assistance administered by A.I.D. is necessary background. A.I.D. uses three basic forms of aid to work towards most of its objectives: technical assistance, capital assistance, and commodity assistance.[9]

Technical Assistance

Technical assistance transfers skills and knowledge. U.S. experts may be sent to the developing country to advise on policies and programs in their fields of specialization and to train host country counterparts ultimately to take over the job. Students, technicians, and officials from the developing country are also brought to the United States (or, sometimes, to a third country) either for short observation tours or for longer training programs.

Technical assistance accounted for 17 per cent of total A.I.D. dollar commitments in fiscal years 1965 and 1966. However, a much larger share—in fact, the great majority—of A.I.D. *staff* abroad and

[8] *Ibid.,* p. 12.
[9] For a more detailed discussion of these forms of aid plus information on additional instruments used by A.I.D., see Agency for International Development, *Principles of Foreign Economic Assistance,* revised edition, Washington, September 1965, Chapter III.

in Washington are engaged in providing technical assistance directly or in providing administrative and technical support for such assistance.

Capital Assistance

Capital assistance supports creation, expansion, and modernization of capital, that is, of the concrete physical means of production (factories, roads, ports, power facilities, irrigation works, grain storage facilities) as well as physical facilities that are essential to an efficient economy but that make their contribution to production indirectly (communications facilities, schools, potable water systems). Most developing countries need more imports for capital investment plus consumption than they can pay for from their exports. Private investment from abroad may cover part but seldom all of the gap. Capital assistance [10] finances the remainder.

Most capital assistance is provided for specific projects—a fertilizer factory, loading equipment for a port, a library or laboratory equipment for a university. The borrower may be the government of the aided country, an institution such as a university, or a private firm. The donor can examine the plans for the project and make sure that they are sound before agreeing to provide financing. The receiving party usually pays for all or a substantial part of the local costs of labor and locally available material.

But reviewing individual projects is costly and time-consuming. Therefore capital assistance is sometimes provided through development banks, which act as "retailers." In other words, the donor lends to a development bank within a developing country. The bank in turn undertakes to use the funds to finance sound projects, usually privately owned, and assumes responsibility for selecting and administering the loan projects. The donor assesses the reliability of the bank, but does not examine individual projects except on a spot-check basis.

Capital assistance absorbed a quarter of A.I.D. commitments in fiscal year 1965, and 16 per cent in 1966. Because the volume of capital assistance depends largely on the flow of sound project proposals from governments and private firms, the level may fluctuate substantially from year to year.

Commodity Assistance

Commodity assistance finances imports for an economy as a whole, to permit it to operate more fully and efficiently. The process

---

[10] Plus commodity assistance, discussed in the next section.

of growth creates demands for imported raw materials and equipment, which are not associated with construction of specific new projects, but are needed to permit *existing* factories to operate at full capacity or to introduce a double or triple shift; to make it possible for private firms to modernize and expand; to supply farmers with fertilizers and pesticides, which the extension agents have taught them are necessary to increase crop yields but which are not yet produced in the country itself; to provide the fuel and parts needed by railroads and trucks to meet growing demands.

Financing construction of new projects cannot meet this kind of development requirement. The efficient way to respond to such needs is to provide funds against which imports from the donor can be credited, and to let the market system determine the precise composition of the imports. Tariffs, duties, quantitative restrictions, and licensing controls may be used to prevent luxury imports and to give priority to key development industries. However, in order to have confidence that a "program loan," as it is called in A.I.D., will indeed support developmental needs, one must have confidence in the policies and administration of the receiving country's government.

Under different circumstances, for example, in a country like Vietnam, commodity imports serve to bolster an economy that could not otherwise maintain large defense forces and meet civilian needs without uncontrollable inflation. Still different might be the case of the government that does not bear a heavy defense burden but, due to the failure of a major export crop or to problems inherited from a previous regime or to its own incompetence, faces an acute foreign exchange or budget crisis. Commodity aid directly eases a foreign exchange crisis by providing the imports that the country's depleted foreign exchange reserves cannot finance. Aid can also temporarily ease budget problems. Aid-financed imports are sold to consumers and firms within the aid-receiving country, and the proceeds of the sales (or taxes thereon) provide revenues to help the government finance essential services and programs. Thus commodity aid may be used for straight development requirements, for defense support, or for budget and balance of payments support during temporary crises.

In fiscal 1965, half of total A.I.D. commitments financed commodity assistance. In 1966 the share increased to 59 per cent, primarily reflecting more than doubled imports to Vietnam, plus a substantial increase in commodity assistance for India.

Food aid provided under the Food for Peace program is a special case of commodity aid, financed outside the A.I.D. program. Food for Peace legislation authorizes sales of U.S. agricultural commodities—until autumn 1966, exclusively surplus commodities—for dollars or for the purchaser's own currency. Some of the proceeds from these sales—normally 20 per cent [11]—is set aside to pay for U.S. Government expenditures within the buying nation, for example, costs of maintaining the Embassy. The remainder of the proceeds is usually loaned back to the buyer on easy terms, for developmental or other specified uses. Food for Peace commodities may also be donated for relief, school lunch, food-for-work, and similar programs, which are often administered by private U.S. voluntary agencies working abroad.

In the past few years food aid under the Food for Peace program has come to $1.5 to 1.7 billion annually, while annual A.I.D. obligations have ranged from approximately $2.1 billion (in fiscal years 1964 and 1965) to $2.6 billion (in fiscal year 1966).[12] Funds for the Food for Peace program are separately appropriated, and A.I.D. shares responsibility for their administration with the Department of Agriculture. In autumn 1966 new legislation was passed converting Food for Peace from a program basically oriented toward disposal of surplus U.S. agricultural commodities to an active instrument of foreign aid. While previous criteria guiding Food for Peace were rather different from those followed in A.I.D. programs, the two should now become quite closely integrated.

A.I.D. also administers a variety of additional programs individually authorized and funded by Congress, such as contributions to international organizations and investment guaranties designed to encourage private investors to invest in the developing countries. However, the basic forms of aid that constitute the core of the A.I.D. program are technical assistance, capital projects, and commodity imports. Different amounts and combinations of these three basic forms of aid, plus adjustments in the timing and conditions of aid, delaying or withholding of aid, and use of access to host country officials for discussion and persuasion, permit aid to be used as a flexible and often powerful instrument of U.S. foreign policy.

[11] Congress establishes a minimum proportion of total worldwide sales (not necessarily applicable in each individual country) which must be set aside for U.S. uses. This minimum was increased from 10 to 20 per cent effective in 1966.

[12] A.I.D., *U.S. Overseas Loans and Grants*, 1945–1965, p. 5, and *Operations Report*, FY 1966.

Part One: A.I.D. GOALS AND PROGRAMS

CHAPTER 1

Aid Purposes

BECAUSE ECONOMIC ASSISTANCE is an instrument of the full range of U.S. interests in the developing countries, a statement of these interests is a logical starting point for a survey of aid uses. Four major strands of U.S. interest in the developing countries are clear:

1. Standard interests, which apply to relations with any country: protection of U.S. citizens and property, and equal access with other nations to opportunities for trade and investment.
2. A set of fairly specific concerns arising from the Cold War: continued access to military bases and other strategic facilities located in specific developing countries; maintaining ties with formal allies and strengthening their defense capacity; delaying recognition of Communist China and its admission to the United Nations; discouraging trade, particularly in strategic goods, with Communist China, Cuba, and North Vietnam; more generally, encouraging independence or a pro-Western alignment in the foreign policy positions of developing countries.
3. A set of interests that have become entangled with Cold War concerns, but spring from a historically earlier and separate desire to encourage evolution of a responsible international community in which conflicts are resolved through peaceful channels and nations cooperate on economic, scientific, and other mutually beneficial programs. These interests are reflected in support for U.N. peacekeeping missions; in separate U.S. actions intended to forestall or halt violence and resolve disputes (for example, between Turkey and Greece in Cyprus, between India and Pakistan, between Indonesia and Malaysia);

support for regional organizations such as the Organization of American States, the Economic Commission for Africa, and the Asian Development Bank, and for subregional groupings like the Regional Organization for Central America and Panama and the East African Common Services Organization; and support for programs cutting across national boundaries, such as the development of the Indus River basin, which serves India and Pakistan, and development of the Mekong River basin in Southeast Asia.

4. Finally, a concern for the pace and pattern of internal economic and political evolution in the developing countries. This concern is fed, to varying degrees at different times, by humanitarian desire to ease and ultimately conquer poverty; by Cold War-stimulated fear of successive Communist takeovers in the less-developed world; and by the recognition that even in the absence of the Communist threat, the tensions caused by rising expectations, population growth, and economic and social change already under way would pose a threat to internal progress and international stability throughout the underdeveloped world, hence to the emergence of an international community in which the United States can live in peace and prosperity.

In practice, U.S. concern for the internal evolution of the developing countries usually focuses most directly and immediately on their economic growth. But it is far from obvious to all observers that economic progress in Latin America, Africa, and Asia will serve important U.S. interests. Certainly there is no necessary connection between economic growth and internal political stability. Indeed, at least in early stages growth and change are likely to accentuate instability by disrupting traditional social and political relations and institutions and disorienting and frustrating important groups. Similarly, it is naive to presume that growth and democracy go hand in hand. Much of the recent literature on political development suggests the need for centralization of power as a first requisite for national integration and adoption of modernizing reforms.[1] Finally, neither economic progress nor democratic forms of government have prevented nations in the past from initiating or provoking wars.

[1] See, for example, Samuel P. Huntington, "The Political Modernization of Traditional Monarchies," *Daedalus,* Vol. XCV, No. 3, Summer 1966, p. 768, and "Political Modernization: America vs. Europe," *World Politics,* Vol. XVIII, No. 3, April 1966, pp. 410–412.

What basis is there, then, to believe that economic progress in the developing countries serves long-run U.S. interests? I will only summarize the argument here, since it has been stated elsewhere clearly and, in my opinion, persuasively.[2] The U.S. interest in assisting economic growth rests on the following premises: that unrelieved poverty and frustration will breed extremism, which domestic and foreign groups will be quick to exploit; that most men, given fair prospects for material improvement and a sense of growing dignity and acceptance in their community and nation, will not resort to extreme or violent solutions to their problems; that education, mobility, and participation in such institutions as cooperatives or credit unions will build capacity for responsible political participation; that a nation whose leaders and citizens are absorbed in internal development programs is less likely to look for scapegoats or for national prestige through foreign adventures than a nation that is stagnant or chaotic; that a politically united and economically strong nation is both less likely to be the object of external intervention or subversion than a divided and weak nation, and more able to participate constructively in the international community; and that growing wealth and diversity of economic interests in the developing countries will offer broadened opportunities for trade and investment. Thus, in the long run, development is expected both to increase international and internal stability and to help create conditions for a mutually beneficial community of nations.

Regardless of what the United States does or does not do, the processes of change are under way in every nation of the less-developed world. The U.S. interest in promoting growth is a calculated gamble that by speeding the process, easing the degree of sacrifice required, and urging concomitant social and political reform, the benefits of growth may be more quickly and widely felt and the odds in favor of stability and democratic evolution enhanced.

There is also a strong humanitarian basis for the U.S. interest in promoting economic growth. U.S. income per person in 1965 was $3,476. Average income per person in Asia is estimated at $87; in Africa south of the Sahara it is $100.[3] This is a ratio of roughly 35 to 1. Yet the statistics, striking as they are, fail to convey the real

[2] See, for example, Max F. Millikan, "The Political Case for Economic Development Aid," in Robert A. Goldwin, ed., *Why Foreign Aid?*, Rand McNally, Chicago, 1963.

[3] *Statistical Abstract of the United States,* 1966, p. 323, and A.I.D., Statistics and Reports Division, "Estimates of Gross National Product," February 18, 1966.

gap to most of us. It takes a stretch of the imagination to grasp what it means to live on less than $100 a year.[4] The trends are even more appalling than the static comparisons. The gap between rich and poor nations is growing, not narrowing. In some of the largest poor nations, food production has not kept pace with accelerating population growth: less food per person is produced now than a few years ago. For many, the moral challenge of these facts is a more persuasive case for the U.S. interest in encouraging economic growth abroad than is the argument from enlightened self-interest.

How does U.S. economic aid support these foreign policy objectives? Briefly, most of it is used for two purposes: to accelerate long-term economic and social development, and to contribute directly and immediately to the security of nations in imminent danger of disintegration into chaos, insurgent takeover, or (more in the late 1940's and the early 1950's than at present) external attack. Much smaller amounts of aid are used for various more immediate and specific political or humanitarian purposes.

Developmental Aid

Most A.I.D. efforts—about two thirds of dollar commitments between 1962 and 1967—are designed primarily to accelerate economic growth and social progress in the aided country. On the strictly economic side, economic growth encompasses:

1. Development of technical, professional, entrepreneurial, and managerial skills.
2. Increased productivity and output in industry and agriculture.
3. Diversification of crops and industries, to reduce dependence on one or a few mineral or agricultural exports and consequent vulnerability to world market price fluctuations, and to reduce relative reliance on imported goods. (The absolute quantity of imports will almost certainly rise in any growing economy.)
4. Increased savings and investment, to the point where self-financed investment plus foreign private investment permits output to grow faster than population.
5. Increased exports, to the point where export earnings plus foreign private investment can finance sufficient imports for both consumption and investment.

[4] This is precisely the purpose of pages 33 to 37 of Eric Heilbronner's book, *The Great Ascent,* Harper & Row, New York, 1963.

The priorities among these goals vary at different stages of development, and the contribution of foreign economic aid also varies with the recipient's level of development. The least developed countries need first to develop basic skills and institutions. Technical assistance —training and advisory services—plays the key role at this stage. Countries at the earliest stages of development also need some capital investment in schools, roads, ports, power, water systems—the physical prerequisites for later growth of industry and modernized agriculture. But construction of such infrastructure should not too far outstrip the country's capacity to maintain and use the new facilities. There is no point in constructing schools for which there are no teachers, or in building roads that will carry little traffic and will deteriorate for lack of adequate maintenance.

Therefore, although the least developed countries would seem to need economic aid most urgently, in fact they cannot use large amounts of aid effectively. Technical assistance is much less expensive than capital assistance. The average annual cost per U.S. advisor is $25,000 to $30,000 (and U.S. advisors are expensive compared to those from other countries). Training persons from the developing countries in the United States costs an average of $5,000 to $6,000 a year plus transportation costs. In contrast, most capital assistance projects are reckoned in millions. Since the "aid package" to a very underdeveloped country should include comparatively high proportions of technical assistance, the total dollar value of aid the country can absorb tends to be low. Moreover, at very early stages of development, even capacity to use technical assistance and participant training is limited. Advisors must have more or less qualified students or counterparts to work with; these are hard to find where college graduates are numbered in tens and high school graduates in hundreds. Similarly, participants sent abroad for study must be at least partially prepared for their programs of study. Theoretically, of course, it would be possible to finance large numbers of operational personnel—professional and technical specialists whose primary task is not to train host country personnel but to perform the job themselves—to staff government services and even productive enterprises. This would amount to a quasi-colonial regime, which would be palatable to neither the United States nor the recipient country. France currently finances thousands of teachers, administrators, and military personnel in most French-speaking African nations. The French expatriates are essential to permit the countries to function, but their number and influence arouse deep resentment. Had this pattern of assistance not been carried over from pre-Independence days, it probably would not have been acceptable at all.

As a country accumulates skills and builds up institutions and infrastructure, the scope for public and private investment in industry and modernized agriculture broadens. Building and operating factories and introducing modern farming techniques require equipment and materials the country does not yet produce. Normally its export earnings are not great enough to cover the foreign exchange costs of importing the equipment and materials. Foreign private investment, while growing, is not large enough to fill the gap. Thus there is substantial need for aid-financed loans for capital projects, and the total amount of aid the country can use effectively increases sharply.

Rapid growth may also generate demands for imported commodities to permit already-established factories and transportation facilities to operate at full capacity and to provide fertilizer, pesticides, and other materials for modernized agricultural production. Such requirements are most efficiently financed through commodity assistance. While the total amount of project lending is limited by the rate at which the recipient country can prepare and donors can review project proposals, commodity assistance is not thus encumbered. Therefore, large amounts of commodity aid can be transferred quickly. Those countries receiving the greatest U.S. economic aid, with the exception of the security-oriented programs in Vietnam and Laos, are all relatively advanced countries whose economies require commodity assistance to maintain rapid growth and whose policies warrant a degree of confidence that such aid will be used productively.

Up to some point, a country's ability to use external funds efficiently for growth increases faster than its ability to earn foreign exchange. But as agricultural and industrial growth become more efficient, diversified, and high-quality, the country is increasingly able to compete in export markets. As future prospects for foreign exchange earnings brighten, the country can also afford to borrow from conventional banking sources of foreign exchange at higher interest rates without assuming an excessive debt burden. Moreover, the country's expanding economy becomes more attractive to foreign private investors who bring with them the foreign exchange needed to start their businesses. For all these reasons, the country's need for capital and commodity assistance on concessional terms [5] tapers off. As its own educational and other institutions gain strength, and

[5] Loan terms (interest rate, repayment period, grace period) are "concessional" if they are more generous than a commercial bank would provide.

as private investors bring in certain kinds of technical skills, the need for technical assistance also dwindles. Eventually, the country reaches the point where it no longer needs concessional assistance of any kind to maintain its economic growth.

The foregoing explains *how* foreign economic aid is used at different stages of development to support further economic growth. But does this not beg the basic question of whether such aid is necessary at all? Professor Edward C. Banfield has argued:

Where cultural conditions do not allow of it, economic development will not take place, no matter how much aid is given. On the other hand, where cultural conditions are right for it, development will occur rapidly in the absence of any aid. Japan and Russia both developed rapidly without aid. No country is too poor to accumulate capital if its people are disposed to save and to invest, and the technical knowledge of the Western world is easily available to the underdeveloped countries—indeed, could not be withheld from them—if they are willing to avail themselves of it.[6]

It is, of course, true that the obstacles to growth are deeply rooted in the cultures, social structures, and political systems of the less-developed countries, as well as in more tangible problems of lack of skills, inadequate institutions, scarce resources, population pressure, and difficult climate and geography. But as Professor Banfield himself goes on to note, there is "an important middle group of countries" that "show fair promise of eventual development" and also plainly cannot progress without substantial aid.[7] Almost all U.S. developmental aid goes to these countries, as explained in Chapter 2. Moreover, it is risky to conclude too hastily that conditions in particular countries preclude growth. In 1960, the idea that Korea might attain self-sustaining growth in the foreseeable future was inconceivable. Yet since 1964 Korea has made such strides that by 1966 both the Korean Government and the U.S. Government were predicting an end to aid within a few years. The little kingdom of Jordan, arid, resource-poor, and faced with the problem of integrating bitter Palestinian refugees numbering a quarter of its population, used to be cited as a classic illustration of a "nonviable economy." Jordan had long depended heavily on foreign subsidies, British before 1957 and American thereafter. Yet determined leadership (plus U.S. prodding) brought real progress by 1967. In 1960 Jordan financed from domestic revenues only 45 per cent of her expenditures. In 1966, despite increased

---

[6] Edward C. Banfield, "American Foreign Aid Doctrines," in Goldwin, ed., *Why Foreign Aid?, op. cit.,* pp. 12–13.

[7] *Ibid.*

spending for development, she financed two-thirds of her budget. Moreover, before the Arab-Israeli War of June 1967, the Jordanian economy was growing rapidly.[8] Even the grave setbacks resulting from the war are not likely to revive the prediction of perennial dependence.

Many nations of Africa and Asia, and some in Latin America, face decades before they can hope to be self-sustaining. Aid's role is marginal. It cannot create—though it can encourage—conditions essential for growth. But a long time is not never, and a marginal contribution may, at a critical juncture, make the difference between progress and stagnation.

The discussion to this point has concerned economic growth alone. But economic progress is inextricably entangled with politics and social change. Moreover, even if it were feasible to divorce economic growth from political and social progress, U.S. interests go well beyond the creation of modern, self-sustaining economies. Additional goals are:

1. A more equitable distribution of wealth, income, services, and opportunity among classes, regions, and ethnic groups, and between urban and rural areas.
2. Progress toward a system of government that is stable enough to encourage development, reasonably responsive to public aspirations, capable of promoting broadened political participation, and tolerant of dissent within broad limits.

While these goals are as important as—some would argue more important than—more strictly economic objectives, in general we know less about how to encourage political and social progress than about how to overcome economic or technical problems. Moreover, although most developing countries will accept some foreign advice on economic and technical questions, they are more likely to resent and resist what they view as intervention in their political and social affairs. For these and other reasons, the United States has given less explicit attention and emphasis to these goals than to economic objectives.

Nonetheless, many A.I.D. activities increase the welfare or improve the bargaining position of disadvantaged groups, thereby increasing equity—for example, adult literacy campaigns, village school self-help programs, intensive assistance programs for isolated

[8] A.I.D., *Gross National Product: Growth Rates and Trend Data,* March 31, 1967.

and neglected regions of particular countries, training for labor union leaders. A.I.D. has also pressed for reforms in land tenure, tax structure, educational priorities, and other host government measures, which will increase equity as well as promoting growth.

Very little U.S. economic aid contributes directly to broadened political participation and more responsive governments. A.I.D. generally takes an indirect approach to these goals, hoping that more and better education, widespread experience in organizations like cooperatives and credit unions, and the emergence of a landed peasantry and a commercial and technical middle class will contribute in turn to broadened and responsible political participation. But in some countries U.S. economic aid may not have strengthened democratic trends, and may even have consolidated the strength of conservative elites. A.I.D. makes almost no effort to assess aid's long-term impact, whether intended or accidental, on the political structure and evolution of recipient countries.

For years some people both within and outside the agency have urged a more active effort to promote political development. Recently Congress has instructed A.I.D. to design its programs so as to encourage the development of democratic institutions. It is obvious that democracy does not follow automatically from economic progress, but it is less clear how much and what can be done to improve the chances of democratic evolution.

Aid to Establish Security and Stability

In the long run, developmental aid is expected to increase the stability of the new nations and the security of the United States. Secretary of Defense Robert S. McNamara stated this view particularly clearly in May 1966, using data showing a striking correlation between poverty and instability, and concluding:

Roughly 100 countries today are caught up in the difficult transition to modern societies. . . . This sweeping surge of development has no parallel in history. It has turned traditionally listless areas of the world into seething cauldrons of change. On the whole, it has not been a very peaceful process. . . . The years that lie ahead for the nations in the southern half of the globe are pregnant with violence. This would be true even if no threat of Communist subversion existed—as it clearly does. . . . Whether Communists are involved or not, violence anywhere in a taut world transmits sharp signals through the complex ganglia of international relations; and the security of the United States *is* related to the security and stability of nations half a globe away.

The Secretary hastened to add that he did not suggest the United States could or should become the "Global Gendarme." But since growth appears to be essential (though not necessarily sufficient) for security, the United States should support development efforts in those countries that need and request assistance, and are demonstrably able and willing to help themselves.[9]

Thus developmental aid, if it is successful, is expected ultimately to promote increased stability within and among nations. But long-run economic and social progress is no answer to immediate and severe internal insurgency or external attack. Therefore, economic aid is also used, often in conjunction with military aid, to try to ward off imminent violence or to cope with it once it has occurred. Between 1961 and 1966 roughly a fifth of A.I.D. funds was spent to address immediate security problems. Recently the intensified war in Vietnam has claimed a much larger share of U.S. aid.

During the 1950's, a good part of U.S. economic assistance, as well as military aid, went to increase defense capabilities in countries on the southern and eastern borders of the Soviet Union and Communist China. Military assistance is the most obvious means of helping a country prepare for—and thereby, perhaps, prevent—threatened external attack. But maintaining large defense forces strains a country's total economy. It often calls for a local defense budget in excess of the government's ability to raise tax revenues, and creates inflationary pressures. In countries where the United States has felt it important to support a major defense effort—at different times in Greece, Turkey, Iran, Pakistan, Taiwan, Korea, Vietnam—economic assistance has been used to finance commodity imports that increase the supply of goods people want to buy, thereby easing inflationary pressure. Moreover, the imports are sold within the recipient country, and the proceeds (or taxes on the proceeds) can be used by the recipient government to increase its defense budget.

Outside Southeast Asia, the need for economic aid to strengthen countries against external attack has diminished greatly since 1960. Soviet and Communist Chinese emphasis has shifted from overt aggression to support for internal subversive movements. Moreover, several of the countries bordering the Soviet Union or China are increasingly able to maintain both sizeable defense forces and energetic development programs while A.I.D. assistance is reduced or

[9] Address by Secretary of Defense Robert S. McNamara before the American Society of Newspaper Editors, Montreal, Canada, May 18, 1966. Italics taken from the original.

eliminated. Greece and Taiwan have received no A.I.D. assistance for several years; both sustain sizeable armed forces and are making good economic progress. (Military aid and Food for Peace assistance to both countries has continued.) In Iran, oil revenues permit substantial military and development expenditures without foreign assistance.

However, the threat of internal unrest and insurgency in many of the developing countries has not diminished. In some, it has increased. Domestic Communist agitation and, in some instances, foreign Communist supplies of arms and men may aggravate these internal security threats, but the original tensions are homegrown. Tribal hostility was the clear basis for the disintegration of law and order and the outbreak of armed rebellion in the Congo in the early 1960's and in Nigeria in 1966, although foreign Communist and other groups did provide arms to the Congolese rebels. Disaffection in the Dominican Republic was rooted in social and economic grievances.

U.S. economic assistance is used both to help governments maintain the forces to suppress insurgents, and to help remove some of the causes of the insurgency. If active widespread rebellion or insurgency has already occurred, as in the Congo in 1961 or in Laos and Vietnam, economic aid serves as did "defense support" programs of the 1950's to combat inflation and support larger defense budgets by financing imported consumer and producer goods. Commodity import programs currently account for much of our economic assistance to Laos and Vietnam. Economic aid is also used for roads, communications facilities, and airstrips, which serve both development and security purposes, and for equipment such as portable radio transmitters for Vietnamese villagers to summon help against guerrilla attack. While military assistance provides equipment, military supplies, and advisors for the armed forces, economic assistance is used to equip, provision, train, and advise paramilitary forces such as the police and border patrols.

To a large extent the violence in Laos and Vietnam is guerrilla warfare rather than conventional open warfare. An effective defense against conventional attack is likely to force the insurgents to fall back upon guerrilla tactics.[10] Successful control of guerrilla warfare demands the active cooperation of the local people. Therefore economic aid is also used for relief and quick-impact development programs designed to benefit promptly and win the support of villagers. In Vietnam, A.I.D. has Provincial Representatives in each of the

[10] See Brian Crozier, *The Rebels,* Beacon Press, Boston, 1960, pp. 127–129.

43 provinces, directing programs including refugee relief, agricultural extension, construction of schools and clinics, and hundreds of other activities.

In certain other countries, while there is no active insurgency under way, disaffection in particular regions threatens future stability. Northeast Thailand, for example, traditionally has been isolated from the remainder of the country. Its people are related ethnically to the Lao rather than the Thai. It is desperately poor and has not shared in the progress of the rest of the country. In the past few years infiltration and agitation have aggravated traditional alienation. In Brazil, the isolated and poverty-stricken Northeast has been a perennial problem. Recently, disaffection has flared into widespread protest. On the Peruvian Altiplano (high plateau), Indians traditionally scorned and ignored by the people of Lima and the coast scratch a bare living from a bleak environment. In the past few years agitators have begun to convert economic and social grievances into political protest and violence.

To provide concrete evidence of progress in such regions and to create a sense of a stake in the nation, A.I.D. has financed large multifaceted programs emphasizing activities that have quick and widely felt benefits. In April 1962 the United States and Brazil signed a two-year agreement in which both governments pledged special efforts to alleviate the poverty and misery of Northeast Brazil. Aid was concentrated on health, elementary and secondary education, potable water, sewerage, highways, and power facilities. In Northeast Thailand, intensive U.S.-assisted Thai government programs in health, primary education, agricultural extension, community development, and civic education (with a substantial element of patriotic indoctrination) are concentrated in those provinces most threatened by subversion. Indeed, most U.S. economic aid to Thailand focuses on the Northeast; the remainder of the country is making good progress without foreign assistance. Improved communications may also help to integrate a region with the remainder of the country, making it easier for the central government to extend both services and control into the region and for cash crops to find a market in the remainder of the country. In Northeast Thailand, A.I.D. has helped finance hundreds of miles of all-weather roads designed to further both security and economic integration.

These efforts are concerned with both development and short-run security. The emphasis depends on the intensity of the security threat.

In Northeast Thailand, where the threat is imminent and associated with the broader international conflict, emphasis on security is strong. In Northeast Brazil, where the threat is viewed as serious but less imminent, more stress is placed on somewhat longer-run development efforts.

Economic aid is also used to counter smaller-scale, more scattered threats to a nation's security and stability, as well as to help control widespread insurgency and to reduce regional disaffection. For example, Colombia and Venezuela do not face widespread, large-scale insurgency, but are plagued with scattered bandit and terrorist groups seeking, at least in part, political ends. In both countries the United States finances sizeable programs to train and equip the police. (Smaller police training programs are conducted in many other countries, but where there is no significant security threat, such aid is simply intended to strengthen a basic governmental service, much like other public administration assistance.) On occasion, governments have requested and the United States has provided special riot control equipment to forestall expected disturbances or to cope with them once they have occurred.

Aid to Influence Internal Politics or Foreign Policies

Although long-run, developmental aid may improve (not guarantee) the chances of political development and democratic evolution, such aid cannot address immediate political crises, just as it fails to cope with immediate threats to a nation's security. Therefore, economic aid is used in a variety of ways to try to influence the current political situation in the aided country, where the outcome appears important to more lasting U.S. interests.

For example, economic aid has been used in Brazil, the Dominican Republic, Guyana, and elsewhere to buy time for new regimes to consolidate their positions and formulate programs of action. New regimes often inherit overwhelming budget or foreign exchange deficits, sometimes accompanied by runaway inflation. An injection of commodity imports can provide a breathing space during which the government can draw up programs to address the causes of the problems. Occasionally commodity imports are also used to help an already-established government out of an economic crisis. Such emergency aid may indicate active support for the regime and the belief that it will use the time so bought to correct the causes of the crisis, or simply the conviction that the alternatives to the present government are chaos or extremism.

Economic problems short of a general economic crisis, for example, unemployment concentrated in a particular region or age group, may also represent a political threat, which foreign aid can help to ease. In Kenya demonstrations and riots by unemployed young men in their teens and early twenties led the Government of Kenya to create and A.I.D. to assist a voluntary National Youth Service somewhat like the Civilian Conservation Corps of the depression years in the United States.

Economic assistance has also been used to try to influence the outcome of elections, or simply to ensure that the elections are held. In Venezuela terrorists sought to sabotage the elections of autumn 1963, warning that those who went to the polls would be marks for snipers. The United States stepped up support for the Venezuelan military and police. Where pre-election pressures have caused a government to relax unpopular controls or policies, resulting in inflation, unrest, and a handicap for moderate candidates, the United States has more than once tried to redress the balance by financing commodity imports to dampen inflation and restore confidence. Economic assistance has also been withheld from half a dozen Latin American countries after military coups to demonstrate U.S. disapproval and to encourage early scheduling of elections and a return to constitutional government.

Economic aid is also used, along with diplomacy and other foreign policy instruments, to try to influence recipients' foreign policy views —their attitudes toward the United States, their Cold War role, and their behavior toward their neighbors and in international organizations outside a Cold War context.

Perhaps the most obvious of these objectives is good will toward the United States. U.S. interest in good will is not simply a manifestation of American desire to be liked. Good will and diplomatic access are the prerequisites without which U.S. influence on more specific issues will be limited. Ideally all economic aid should promote good will. But in practice, of course, the very fact of dependence on assistance may produce resentment. Moreover, the complex regulations and procedures that A.I.D. requires and the self-help conditions that are often attached to developmental aid are irritating under the best circumstances. Therefore, in most countries where A.I.D. conducts substantial programs, good will per se is a marginal objective. Certain standard arrangements are made to publicize the source of the aid,[11] thereby hopefully ensuring recognition and encouraging good will, but in general, projects are not selected or designed on grounds of how much good will they will create.

Sometimes, however, projects or even whole country programs are undertaken primarily to create good will for the United States. Independence Day gifts, the Mission Director's Fund for use at his discretion to support small self-help projects, "pet" projects ardently desired by heads of state or other key political figures despite a low development priority, and showy "impact" projects are all designed to advertise U.S. generosity and interest in the recipient nation. And in a number of small sub-Saharan African nations where other donors finance most of the development aid required, the United States provides limited amounts of technical and capital assistance largely to demonstrate U.S. friendship and encourage reciprocal feelings.

Turning from good will to more concrete aspects of bilateral relations between recipient nations and the United States, economic aid is used to protect U.S. economic and military interests. By law,[12] aid to a nation that nationalizes or expropriates U.S. public or private property without adequate compensation is suspended, as in Ceylon from 1963 to mid-1965. When Peru seemed on the verge of expropriating a major U.S. firm, A.I.D. loans were delayed to pressure the government to negotiate its differences with the firm. In several countries economic aid was formerly used to pay explicit rental for military bases, but it is no longer so used. There are still, however, U.S. economic aid programs which are larger than they would be were strategic facilities not located in the recipient countries.

Economic aid is also enlisted to serve short-run Cold War aims. Countries that permit ships or aircraft under their registry to carry goods to Cuba or North Vietnam are not eligible for economic, military,[13] or (as of autumn 1966) food aid.[14] In a few cases the promise of aid has been used as a bribe to induce a country to refuse overflight and landing rights to the Soviet Union or to delay recognition of Communist China.

A considerably more important Cold War purpose is to prevent

---

[11] A.I.D.-financed capital projects must be clearly identified as such by a plaque or marker. Food for Peace commodities and trucks and equipment imported under A.I.D. programs are labeled with the "clasped hands" emblem. Wide newspaper and radio coverage is sought for announcements of new aid and dedication of completed projects.

[12] Foreign Assistance Act of 1961 as amended, Section 620(e).

[13] Foreign Assistance Act of 1961 as amended, Section 620(p).

[14] Food for Peace Act of 1966, Section 103(d) (3).

developing nations from relying on Communist aid, where such reliance seems likely to lead to internal subversion or alignment with Soviet bloc or Chinese foreign policy positions. Such "counter-Communist" efforts may take the form of full-scale country assistance programs, as in Guinea until November 1966, or of more limited attempts to maintain Western contact and influence with key groups (police) or fields (mass media, education).

Aside from the Cold War context, aid (or the withholding of aid) is also used to encourage peaceful resolution of disputes. Aid has been cut or withheld to discourage aggression: thus, in an unsuccessful effort to dissuade Sukarno from his confrontation policy toward Malaysia, aid to Indonesia dropped from roughly $120 million (including Food for Peace commitments) in 1963 to zero in 1965.[15] Aid to India and Pakistan was suspended during their border war of 1965–1966.

It is true that the unintended—though often predictable—result of U.S. aid in a number of countries has been to increase their ability to attack or threaten their neighbors. Military assistance can be and has been so diverted, despite provisions in the aid agreements stipulating that the equipment provided be used only for defense. This has happened in the Greek-Turkish confrontation over Cyprus and in the Indo-Pakistan conflict. Ethiopia has used U.S.-supplied airplanes to bomb and strafe border areas of Somalia. Economic aid can have a similar effect indirectly, by permitting a country to divert more of its own resources to military use without sacrificing developmental goals. The United States has often been shortsighted in failing to anticipate such consequences of its aid.

Aid is also used in quite a different way to support and encourage international cooperation, through development of effective and responsible regional and subregional organizations. Both capital and technical assistance have gone to regional institutions like the Economic Commission for Africa and to subregional groupings such as the Regional Organization for Central America and Panama and the East Africa Common Services Organization.

Humanitarian Aid

Finally, some economic aid goes for purely humanitarian purposes. The two clearest types of humanitarian aid are disaster relief and

---

[15] A.I.D., *U.S. Overseas Loans and Grants, 1945–1965,* p. 62.

support for the relief programs conducted by private U.S. charitable organizations abroad.

Every U.S. Ambassador or Chief of Mission has authority to use up to $25,000 for relief for victims of disasters such as flood, earthquake, volcanic eruption, hurricane, drought and famine, landslide, or epidemic. The authority applies to each separate instance, so that if a country suffers several disasters in one year, the Ambassador may spend up to $25,000 on relief for each of them. Much larger sums are often used with permission from Washington. Food for Peace commodities is also available for disaster relief. For example, floods and landslides on the steep and heavily populated hills of Rio de Janeiro in January 1966 killed hundreds and left thousands homeless. A total of $72,000 in A.I.D. funds was provided for tents, blankets, and medical supplies and food from Food for Peace supplies was distributed.

Almost five hundred private U.S. agencies provide technical assistance and conduct relief programs in the developing countries. Sixty of these are registered with A.I.D.'s Advisory Committee on Voluntary Foreign Aid. They include organizations such as Church World Service, Catholic Relief Services, the American Jewish Joint Distribution Committee, Inc., CARE, and organizations set up by farm, labor, educational, health, and welfare groups. A.I.D. pays ocean freight to transport books, medicines, used clothing, tools, and other contributions collected in the United States by the voluntary agencies; in fiscal year 1966, this freight bill came to over $5 million.[16] Far greater support for the private agencies is provided through the Food for Peace program. In fiscal year 1965 about $320 million in food and fiber was provided to 17 agencies for use in their overseas programs. That year, food distributed by the voluntary agencies helped feed some 70 million people, including roughly 40 million children reached through school lunch programs.[17]

A.I.D. also provides substantial support for health programs such as the World Health Organization's worldwide malaria eradication drive; the campaign to inoculate all children in 19 West African countries against measles, which there kills as many as a fourth of the children who contract it; and the program to fortify Food for Peace dry milk, flour and cornmeal with vitamins and iron, particularly for preschool children. Such programs serve an obvious humanitarian purpose; in the long run they also contribute to development.

[16] A.I.D., *Operations Report*, FY 1966, p. 22.
[17] A.I.D., *Proposed Economic Assistance Programs*, FY 1967, p. 62.

Aid as a Multipurpose Instrument

Most U.S. economic aid is intended either to promote economic and social progress, or to help restore security and stability in countries where terrorism, insurgency, or external attack are current or imminent. Much smaller sums are used for more immediate political purposes or for humanitarian programs. But each of these general objectives encompasses many more specific goals. Moreover, the U.S. economic assistance program in any one country often is designed to pursue more than one of these objectives.

Nor is there any simple correlation between the form of aid and the primary purpose of specific aid actions. Most technical assistance serves development purposes. But political considerations not infrequently enter into the selection and design of particular projects, and occasionally technical assistance is used for primarily political or security goals. Similarly, both capital projects and commodity imports may serve virtually pure development purposes, almost exclusively political or security goals, or a combination of objectives. However, when A.I.D. finances technical, capital, or commodity assistance for political or security purposes, it normally draws on a special fund called Supporting Assistance, which has been appropriated by Congress specifically for such purposes.

The fact that aid is used to serve so many goals causes confusion and draws criticism at home and abroad. There is broad support among the U.S. public for developmental and humanitarian aid, although many are impatient that the task of development seems to take so long. But aid for political purposes has a nasty ring. Yet specific political uses of aid—for example, withholding aid from military juntas to demonstrate U.S. disapproval—win widespread approval.

Congress is deeply divided regarding the proper goals of foreign aid. Some Congressmen steadfastly support developmental aid to Latin America and, for example, India, but question the value and wisdom of economic aid for security goals. Others heartily approve of aid that seems to serve clear security or stability interests, but challenge pouring millions—indeed, billions—into developmental aid. The disparities within Congress regarding aid priorities are illustrated by Senator Fulbright's and Representative Thomas Morgan's respective views on the wisdom of separating the military assistance and economic assistance bills. From 1962 to 1965, Senator Fulbright, as Chairman of the Senate Foreign Relations Committee, urged that economic assistance legislation be divorced from military assistance bills, while Chairman Morgan (Democrat, Pennsylvania) of the House Foreign Affairs Committee insisted that separating the two programs would cause the economic aid bill to be cut to ribbons. As for using aid to promote immediate political objectives, Congress virtually unanimously condemns the idea in principle, yet is quick to propose using aid for protecting U.S. fishing interests or discouraging trade with Cuba. In the developing countries themselves, the fact that U.S. economic aid is sometimes used to protect U.S. economic interests or to try to influence internal politics or foreign policy positions of recipients is readily interpreted as proof that the entire program is part of a neo-imperialist scheme.

The further question arises whether aid's multiple goals are consistent with each other. There is no simple answer. To a large degree, different uses of aid are complementary. The outcome of an immediate political crisis within an aid-receiving country may be crucial for its long-term development prospects. Reasonable security and stability are prerequisites for economic and social progress, and in some circumstances evidence of such progress may be an essential ingredient in re-establishing security and stability.

But not infrequently, foreign policy purposes for which aid is an instrument conflict. Desire to maintain cordial diplomatic relations, or concern for a regime's stability, or interest in maintaining access to a military installation may inhibit U.S. efforts to promote reform. Conversely, insistence on development criteria may interfere with effective use of aid for short-run political goals. The manner in which aid is used in one country may also affect U.S. interests in other countries. Military aid that stimulates an arms race is an obvious example. Less obvious is the disincentive effect that U.S. crisis support for an inept regime may have in neighboring countries. If the United States is willing to come to the aid of a government that has failed to take needed measures to avoid a budget or foreign exchange crisis, others may well conclude that they need not undertake painful reforms to qualify for aid.

In Ethiopia, for example, the United States has sought simultaneously to maintain the right to operate an important military communications center, to encourage modernizing forces in a country where feudal authority is still strong, and to damp down the long smoldering border dispute with Somalia. Military aid is a quid pro quo for the communications center. But strengthened Ethiopian military forces may threaten the precarious truce with Somalia, and may divert a growing portion of the budget from development uses. Moreover, U.S. arms aid to Ethiopia is a major cause for Somalia's heavy reliance on Communist arms aid. On the economic side, substantial reforms are prerequisites for real progress. Yet too vigorous support for modernizing groups may antagonize others whose good will is essential for maintaining access to the communications center. On the other hand, modernizing groups may be expected to grow more powerful and apparent U.S. support for conservative forces may jeopardize future good relations.

Some conflict among objectives is inevitable. However, there is a strong tendency in the Executive Branch not only to gloss over conflicts among goals in defending proposed or actual actions before Congress and the public, but also to minimize such conflicts in its own deliberations. Sometimes conflicts are transitory, and muddling through may be preferable to borrowing trouble, that is, to anticipating problems which may not materialize. Often, however, obscuring a potential conflict increases the chances that it will occur. Franker appraisal of relations among objectives and more effort to anticipate the side-effects of programs would be feasible and almost surely useful.

CHAPTER 2

Allocation Criteria and Types of Country Programs*

U.S. ECONOMIC AID PROGRAMS are a veritable menagerie of sizes and shapes, reflecting both the wide range of U.S. interests they serve and the tremendous variation in the aided countries' own circumstances.

Criteria for Allocating Aid

Three basic criteria largely determine the volume and content of U.S. economic assistance in any particular country. These are the political importance to the United States of the country's stability and growth; the ability of the country to absorb external resources for growth; and the availability to the country of resources on appropriate terms from other sources.

Importance to the United States

No single factor determines the importance to the United States of another country's stability and growth. The country's size, population, location, and resources clearly are taken into account.

Any special historic tie a country may have with the United States is likely to affect the U.S. Government's view of its importance. The long-standing U.S. interest in Latin America is reflected in the special status of the Alliance for Progress and in separate authorization and appropriation of loan and grant funds for Latin America within the annual Foreign Assistance Acts. Liberia has been viewed historically as the African ward of the United States, dating from its colonization in the early nineteenth century by freed slaves from America. A sense of special responsibility plus concern that lack of progress in Liberia would reflect unfavorably on the United States has led to very high per capita aid for Liberia for over a decade. (The presence of substantial private U.S. interests in Liberia probably is a less influential

---

* This chapter is based on ideas developed within the Program Coordination Staff of A.I.D. in 1963 and 1964. These ideas were used then and later in Agency publications and testimony before Congress.

factor; similar interests in, for example, Zambia have not led to a sizeable aid program there.) The special U.S. interest in Israel led to generous economic assistance from the time the nation was created; domestic U.S. political considerations caused us to continue economic aid for several years after Israel's own savings, export earnings, and ability to attract foreign private investment and support were adequate for both defense and growth.

Ties of military alliance enter into the judgment of a country's importance to the United States, and affect priorities for economic as well as military assistance. Past aid to Greece, Iran, and Taiwan, and current aid to Turkey reflect this factor.

The country's role in regional and international affairs is also considered. Thus substantial U.S. support for Tunisia, which is not large, resource-rich, nor especially strategic, largely reflects Tunisia's constructive role in North African affairs, as well as the hope that her responsible and energetic development efforts might provide a model for other nations. Jordan's role in moderating and balancing Middle Eastern tensions led the United States to provide considerable aid. A nation's strong influence in regional affairs may be grounds for maintaining ties and providing assistance despite discourtesy or periodic hostility, which otherwise would warrant discontinuing aid. Thus modest A.I.D. assistance and more substantial Food for Peace aid for the United Arab Republic have been continued, while aid to Congo (Brazzaville) was suspended in 1964 following a series of unpleasant incidents, and aid to Yemen was withdrawn in May 1967 under somewhat similar circumstances.

A country's internal political orientation also affects the importance to the United States of its stability and growth. Substantial U.S. support for India and Nigeria has reflected not only the size and regional and international importance of both countries, but also (until the tragic events of 1966 and 1967 in Nigeria) the promise both afforded of developing viable, reasonably open, and responsive political systems. In contrast, U.S. distaste for Duvalier's dictatorship in Haiti is evidenced by the fact that the sole aid Haiti receives is a small malaria eradication program; even that might be discontinued but for humanitarian reasons plus the risk to the Dominican Republic, which shares the island.[1] This is not to deny that heavy U.S. aid has gone to nonrepresentative and even repressive regimes. The country's internal political system is one among many factors considered; it can be and often is outweighed by other factors.

[1] *New York Times*, May 9, 1966.

Existing U.S. trade ties and investment in a country, and potential for expanding these, also may influence the judgment of importance to the United States. However, the impact of these considerations is probably less than might be expected. The bulk of U.S. nonoil investment in and trade with the underdeveloped world is concentrated in Latin America. Historic, security, and economic interests combine to give Latin America special priority. The oil-rich nations, while important to the United States, are not candidates for sizeable economic assistance, because their oil revenues can finance their development requirements. The potential for substantial trade and investment in most of the remaining developing nations is far enough in the future so that other U.S. interests tend to dominate decisions regarding aid.

Clearly, there is no formula for weighing these various factors, nor any simple index of "the importance to the United States of a country's continued stability and growth." But a rough judgment of how much it matters to the United States lies behind each decision to stand aloof, put in a token effort, or undertake a sizeable program to prevent disintegration or extremist control, or seriously to promote accelerated economic growth.

Ability to Use Aid Effectively

The second major criterion for allocating aid is the effectiveness with which a country can make use of external resources to accelerate its growth. If a country faces imminent collapse or takeover, the U.S. decision to try to head off disaster or to avoid involvement does not depend on any judgment regarding the country's capacity to use aid to promote growth. But in the absence of such a threat, the United States can weigh whether or not accelerated development in a specific country would significantly advance U.S. interests and how much aid the country can absorb effectively.

Absorptive capacity, like "importance to the United States," has no simple or single index or measure. Some of the more important factors include:

1. Capacity to maintain law and order.
2. Level of development of the country's human resources, including technical, professional, managerial, and entrepreneurial skills.
3. Level of development of its institutional structure, that is, extent and sophistication of credit institutions, extension services,

local government, and private industry, as well as the organization and competence of the central government.

4. Nature and strength of social and cultural obstacles to change, and the extent to which these have become embodied in social organization and political issues.

5. Degree of official commitment to development, as evidenced by efforts to mobilize the country's own resources and to allocate these to the highest priority uses.

Rich natural resources, including favorable soil and climate, obviously make it easier for a country to make effective use of aid for growth. But some countries with good resources have failed to grow for lack of some or all of the other elements listed, while even very resource-poor countries such as Israel have made spectacular progress when other factors were strongly favorable. The factors that determine capacity to use aid effectively correspond closely with the stage of growth a country has already achieved. But at any stage of development, a country's commitment to development and its own self-help efforts strongly affect its further progress and the amount of aid it can absorb.

Availability of Required Resources from Other Sources

The third criterion guiding the allocation of U.S. economic assistance is the availability to a country of resources on appropriate terms from other sources, including other governments, international organizations, and private financiers. "Appropriate terms" refers to the interest rate, period of repayment, and grace period attached to loans. These terms must bear a reasonable relationship to the country's prospects for increased foreign exchange earnings, and to the amount of foreign debt the country already has incurred. Terms that would be appropriate for a country with good earnings prospects and a relatively light debt burden are not appropriate for a country with poorer prospects or heavy obligations already outstanding.

A few fortunate countries can rely on their own resources. Libya is just beginning to modernize. It will probably require foreign advisors and instructors for many decades. But its oil will finance both the salaries of such advisors and the imported equipment and commodities it may need for growth.

Much more commonly, the alternative source of funds is another advanced country, or perhaps a combination of other donor nations and the international agencies that offer development assistance. A geographic division of labor has emerged: the United States provides the great bulk of aid to Latin America; Europe finances most of Africa's development assistance; and the United States, Europe, and Japan all extend substantial aid to various Asian nations. The allocation of U.S. aid takes into account the pattern of other donors' programs. (Where the "other donor" is the Soviet Union, or more broadly the Soviet bloc and/or Communist China, the straight economic calculation may be outweighed by political concern over excessive reliance on Communist sources.)

Terminating aid to a country that has achieved self-sustaining growth is really an application of this third criterion. In other words, the United States has not lost interest in the continued growth of Israel, Greece, and Taiwan, all of which used to receive substantial A.I.D. assistance but now receive none. All three could still put to highly productive use any aid that they were given. But they can now maintain their growth through their own savings and exports, foreign private investment, and borrowing through normal commercial channels such as the Export-Import Bank. Although the interest rates charged by commercial sources are higher than A.I.D. loan terms, the countries' prospective earnings can carry the additional burden of harder terms. Therefore, the United States need not provide more aid to achieve the goal of rapid growth. In some cases, however, the United States has continued to extend small amounts of aid for diplomatic purposes.

To summarize, the amount and composition of U.S. economic aid to any country is roughly determined by that country's importance to the United States, its stage of development and self-help efforts, and its alternative sources of financing. These criteria are imprecise; the first in particular calls for judgments on which there may be great disagreement. Moreover, programs develop their own inertia. The best single clue to how much aid a country will receive next year is how much aid it is receiving this year. But this partly reflects the fact that a country's importance, absorptive capacity, and financial situation rarely change suddenly from one year to another. When a major change in volume or content of aid to a specific country is proposed, the proposal is normally discussed within the U.S. Government in terms of these criteria.

Types of Country Assistance Programs

The purposes, and therefore the design, content, and administration of the U.S. economic assistance programs in different countries vary widely. Any classification of types of country programs is arbitrary, and some individual programs do not fit comfortably into the system. Nonetheless, some grouping is essential if one is to grasp the pattern of the total U.S. economic aid effort. Most of A.I.D.'s country programs can be reasonably described as fitting one of three categories: major development-oriented programs; major programs directed to restoring security and stability; or limited programs directed to narrower goals. This classification is not a system for making decisions, but a description of the results of the decision-making process. In other words, A.I.D. does not classify countries and thereby determine what size and kind of aid program they shall receive. Rather, the basic allocation criteria, country circumstances, and U.S. interests produce the pattern.

Development Programs

In the five years from 1962 through 1966, major development programs were conducted in about 30 countries.[2] Together they received approximately two thirds of total A.I.D. assistance in that period. The primary purpose of U.S. economic assistance to these countries is to accelerate their economic and social progress toward self-sustaining growth.

The 30 countries range widely in their stage of development, from very underdeveloped Liberia to sophisticated Chile. They also vary greatly in the adequacy of their self-help efforts and capacity to use aid effectively to promote growth. The distribution of aid among the 30 reflects these differences. Nine of the countries—Korea, India, Pakistan, Turkey, Nigeria, Tunisia, Brazil, Chile, and Colombia— have generally sound and vigorous self-help records over the past few years. Most are relatively advanced in terms of institutional and industrial structure, technical skills, and administrative competence. All are also important to the United States, because of their size or role in world or regional affairs. Therefore, since 1962 these nine have received the lion's share of A.I.D.'s development funds, and roughly half of all A.I.D. assistance. Moreover, loans for commodity imports make up a large part of A.I.D. assistance to eight of the nine, reflecting substantial confidence in their economic policies and programs. Several can probably reach self-sustaining growth in the next decade.

Smaller development programs are conducted in a number of Latin American countries, the Philippines, and several African nations. In some cases, the relatively small size of the aid program simply reflects the size of the country. For example, on a per capita basis, U.S. assist-

[2] The exact number of countries in each category changed from year to year.

ance to several of the Central American countries has been quite high. However, a number of the countries receiving more modest development assistance have not taken essential reform measures. Comparatively low levels of U.S. assistance to these countries reflect the judgment that they have not demonstrated their capacity to use large-scale aid effectively. As they improve their policies, the United States will probably be willing to provide more aid. A few of the African countries in which the United States conducts moderate-sized development programs also receive substantial aid from other donors. In these countries the scope and volume of U.S. aid is adjusted not only to their stage of development and self-help efforts, but also to take account of other donors' programs.

All the development programs, large and small, go beyond provision of technical and capital assistance to attempt to influence the recipient country's self-help efforts, that is, the composition of its self-financed development programs and the nature of its development policies. Why is such involvement—some would say intervention—necessary? Aid rarely finances more than a small fraction of a country's total development effort. Therefore, what the country does with the remainder of the resources at its disposal will largely determine the pace and pattern of its progress. Moreover, funds are transferable. Aid for any particular project frees some host country resources for other uses (although the donor rarely pays the full costs of any project). The United States may concentrate its aid to a particular country in the fields of education and agriculture; but if the host government gives higher priority to industrial growth and defense, it may shift some of its own resources into these fields. The net effect of U.S. aid to education and agriculture therefore would be increased investment in industry and defense.

In practice, the impact of aid on total resource allocation is seldom completely vitiated. But to make certain that aid has the desired effect on the total pattern of development expenditures in a country, the donor must take an interest in the entire development effort, not solely in those aspects it finances. Therefore, the use of aid to influence host country development efforts is a crucial aspect of effective assistance. Chapter 4 discusses techniques of encouraging more vigorous self-help efforts.

Security Programs

Major programs focused on security and stability problems are conducted in Vietnam, Laos, Thailand, the Congo, the Dominican Republic, and (less clearly), Jordan and Bolivia. From 1962 to 1965, security and stability programs accounted for a fifth of total A.I.D. commitments. In fiscal year 1966, commitments to Vietnam doubled, causing security and stability programs as a group to increase their share to 38 per cent of A.I.D. commitments.

The immediate U.S. objective in these programs is to help the recipient government control insurgency or to alleviate social and economic problems that threaten to explode into violence. The nature of the aid varies with the nature of the problem.

Vietnam and Laos, of course, face large-scale, externally assisted insurrections. U.S. aid to both includes substantial commodity imports to stem inflation and generate sales proceeds to help finance defense budgets. In Vietnam, commodity imports accounted for $507 million out of $590 million in A.I.D. assistance in fiscal year 1966. In Laos, $19 million out of $55 million financed commodity imports.[3] In both, aid is also to improve transportation and communications, to provide immediate relief for refugees, and to bring services and improvements to rural areas, in order to increase their loyalty and willingness to cooperate with their governments. In 1966, A.I.D. financed $80 million in technical assistance for Vietnam,[4] most of which was designed to bring schools, clinics, agricultural extension services, wells, and other services to rural areas. In Laos, A.I.D. supports an intensive rural development program in selected "village clusters" where A.I.D. community development workers and International Voluntary Service workers live and work with Lao counterparts. The program in Laos also includes roughly $10 million a year to airlift rice, hand tools, and other supplies to hundreds of thousands of refugees in remote hill areas.

In Thailand there is no widespread rebellion, but disaffection and infiltration in the Northeast, near the Laotian border, threaten serious trouble. Here U.S. economic aid is almost entirely devoted to improved rural conditions and communications. In the Congo and the Dominican Republic, insurrection has been put down but economic disruption continues. The United States provides large-scale commodity assistance to both countries to prevent inflation and provide operating revenues for the governments. In the Congo, the United Nations and Belgium are taking primary responsibility for rebuilding administrative services. The United States contributes to the United Nations Economic Assistance program for the Congo, and also provides some assistance of this kind directly. In the Dominican Republic, in addition to immedi-

[3] A.I.D., *Operations Report,* FY 1966.
[4] *Ibid.*

ate budget support, we are providing heavy capital and technical assistance to rebuild the economy and get growth under way.

Recognizing Jordan's moderating influence in the Middle East, the United States has subsidized that country's fragile economy for a decade. U.S. assistance in Bolivia has been intended to support the heirs of the thorough-going social revolution of 1952 while preventing its capture by the extreme left. Both Jordan and Bolivia have received substantial budget support; in both, this support has been gradually reduced.

Security programs, then, use the same instruments as developmental programs—technical, capital, and commodity assistance. But technical and capital projects are typically selected to produce quickly felt benefits. And commodity imports are larger-scale, relative to the recipient's economy, than would be true in any development program. For example, the United States, with some assistance from Great Britain, Australia, and other donors, finances virtually all Laotian imports and subsidizes two thirds of the Laotian budget. No development program looms this large relative to the recipient country's total imports and government budget.

By definition, security and stability programs are emergency operations, and often must deal with fragile and overloaded governments. For this reason and because aid's volume relative to the aided country's economy is so large, these programs are extremely difficult to administer and control. Imported goods are pilfered from ships and warehouses and diverted from their intended uses to the black market. Charges of official profiteering are common. And Congressional and public concern is understandably aroused. Yet a massive commodity import program for a country both administratively weak and preoccupied with more threatening problems cannot be conducted without substantial waste. Security and stability programs are expensive; waste is one element of their cost.

Although the immediate objective in security and stability programs is to cope with a current and severe threat, the long-run goal in most of them is development. The judgment that chaos or Communist takeover in a country would gravely harm U.S. interests is analytically distinct from the decision that the country's rapid growth would substantially advance U.S. interests. In practice, however, wherever the United States has intervened in the past to prevent collapse or takeover —in Greece, Turkey, and Taiwan in the late 1940's, in Korea, Jordan, Bolivia, the Dominican Republic—we have soon become involved in major development efforts. Where the threat resulted from internal disaffection, development has been expected to alleviate the causes and prevent a repetition of insurgence. Where the problem was largely or wholly external (Turkey, Taiwan, Korea), development permits continued defense and deterrence while dependence on U.S. aid is gradually reduced.

In Korea, large-scale U.S. aid from the 1953 armistice through the early 1960's primarily financed commodity imports to maintain the economy and support one of the world's largest defense forces. The price of continued military preparedness appeared to be prolonged dependence on the United States. But in the past few years, sound economic policies, high investment rates, rapidly rising savings, and skyrocketing exports have transformed Korea into a promising candidate for self-sustaining growth. The older cases of Greece, Turkey, and Taiwan illustrate still more clearly the evolution from security program to development program to self-sustaining growth. In the late 1940's, all three countries faced severe security threats. Massive U.S. military and economic aid was largely responsible for containing the threat. The countries' own efforts and the focus of U.S. assistance shifted gradually to development. Greece and Taiwan were already relatively advanced in terms of literacy rates, supply of skilled professionals, and business and industrial organization. Both countries adopted sound development policies, and progressed in somewhat over a decade to the point of self-sustaining growth. The last year of A.I.D. assistance to Taiwan was 1963; to Greece, 1964. Turkey started at a somewhat less advanced level, pursued less sound policies, and made slower progress. But in the past few years, Turkey has gained momentum and is now expected to reach self-sustaining growth in the early or mid-1970's.

Similarly, as the budget support component in U.S. aid to Jordan and Bolivia has steadily declined over the past few years, stress on development and self-help has increased. Aid to the Dominican Republic can be expected to focus increasingly on long-run development rather than on immediate relief and stabilization. The United States has announced its readiness to support a large-scale development effort in Southeast Asia as soon as, and to the extent that, security conditions permit.

In a sense, therefore, major security programs and development programs can be viewed as a progression, moving from contained threat to aided growth to self-sustaining growth. The common element is the intention to encourage, through aid, a far-reaching change in the recipient country's internal situation, the enhancement of its capacity to cope with its own needs and problems. Although the content and administration of development and security programs differ substantially, both are change-oriented.

It is striking that among the countries receiving sizeable U.S. assistance, those that have recently achieved or are expected soon to achieve self-sustaining growth are the countries in which U.S. aid was initially and for some years after directed to security problems. The outstanding characteristic of these programs was sustained large-scale commodity assistance. This assistance almost surely served as a powerful catalyst for later rapid growth. Of course, other factors also contributed to rapid progress in these countries. Israel, Greece, Taiwan, and Korea all had relatively well-developed human resources; Israel in particular could draw on large numbers of skilled professional, technical, and managerial personnel. Political events also played a role: reform governments in both Turkey and Korea can claim much credit for the sudden acceleration of growth in the past few years. But it is hard to avoid the conclusion that in these countries sustained, large-scale aid had pump-priming effects—effects that could not be clearly foreseen at the time the assistance was given.

The effectiveness of these security programs in promoting growth may have implications for the conduct of major development-oriented programs. In the absence of a security threat, the United States has been reluctant to provide support on a scale comparable to that of the security programs. Large commodity assistance programs to India and Pakistan are only an apparent exception, because the volume of imports provided is far smaller relative to the size of their economies than is the case in security programs. It may well be that in relatively advanced developing countries, including several in Latin America, U.S. insistence on rather tightly drawn economic criteria for aid has caused us to fall short of our development objectives by restricting the volume of assistance to that for which development uses could be clearly anticipated. More generous assistance, provided with less concern for precise justification of the level, might be more effective.

Limited Objective Programs

The limited objective programs, in contrast to development and security programs, are aimed at much narrower goals, and are not usually change-oriented. The largest group of limited objective programs has been conducted in 19 nations of sub-Saharan Africa, most of them former French colonies. By all of the three allocation criteria, it is appropriate that U.S. assistance to this group be modest in volume and purpose. While several have significant mineral resources, their importance in terms of size, resources, and role in international affairs is limited. They have no historic ties with the United States. Most are at the earliest stages of development. Moreover, they receive substantial assistance from the former colonial powers—France, Belgium, and Great Britain. Average annual per capita assistance from European donors and the international agencies to the French franc area of sub-Saharan Africa is more than twice as high as the average for all developing countries, worldwide.[5]

The U.S. economic assistance programs in countries such as Chad, Dahomey, or Niger are conducted to demonstrate U.S. interest in their progress and thereby strengthen diplomatic ties with them, without supplanting the primary European donor. The programs are too small to have a substantial impact on growth, although most of the individual projects—technical schools, scholarships, road construction equipment—do make a modest contribution to development. Therefore, these programs are informally labeled "presence" or "token" programs. Together they accounted for less than 1 per cent of total A.I.D. outlay in 1966. Most are now being discontinued.

In several of the more advanced Latin American countries, the United States also conducts very small programs with limited objectives. Countries such as Mexico, Venezuela, Jamaica, and Uruguay are able to maintain growth without assistance, although progress in Uruguay has been hampered by inflation and deficit spending. Indeed, Mexico is soon expected to offer technical and capital assistance to Central America. U.S. aid to these countries is intended to encourage progress in specific fields: for instance, low-cost housing and agricultural credit in Mexico; national planning and policy reform in Uruguay; expansion of education and strengthened family planning programs in Jamaica. The modest U.S. programs cannot be interpreted as the phase-out stage of earlier major development support programs, because these countries achieved their level of development before major development assistance was part of U.S. policy in Latin America. The programs can be best understood as symbols of participation in the Alliance for Progress to the limited extent warranted by the countries' needs.

A third group of limited objective programs is directed to countering Soviet or Chinese Communist influence. The program in the Somali

[5] Computed from Organization for Economic Cooperation and Development, *The Flow of Financial Resources to the Less Developed Countries, 1956-1963,* Table II-12, pp. 44–45.

Republic for some years wavered between a large presence program and a small development program. With the influx of massive Soviet military assistance and substantial economic aid in 1964, the U.S. program has taken on a counter-bloc character. In Yemen, which has received $140 million in Soviet and Chinese aid since 1957 for construction of a port, an airport, a road, and military projects, U.S. aid, though developmental in form, was counter-Communist in intent.[6] Aid to Yemen was suspended and the A.I.D. mission was withdrawn in April 1967 following the arrest of two A.I.D. officers on dubious charges that they had tried to blow up an ammunition dump.[7] Afghanistan has long received extensive Soviet aid. The United States has not tried to match or supplant this aid, but has tried to make it clear to the Government of Afghanistan that it does not need to rely exclusively on its northern neighbor for aid, nor, therefore, to tailor its foreign or domestic policies to Soviet preferences. Both donors have selected some of their projects with political implications very much in mind. For example, U.S. aid has financed roads leading to Pakistan and Iran, while USSR-financed roads improve communications to the Soviet border. But in the past few years, U.S. assistance to Afghanistan has focused more strictly on development. As one result, considerably more effort is now made to urge the Government of Afghanistan to improve its development policies and programs. Until November 1966, a fourth counter-Communist program was conducted in Guinea, which had first sought, then turned away from, Soviet assistance to replace withdrawn French support. In November 1966, however, Guinea suddenly expelled the Peace Corps and U.S. Information Service, claiming that the United States Government had been responsible for an incident involving detainment of Guinean diplomats in Ghana; the United States thereupon suspended aid.

A few years ago base-rights programs would have constituted another group of limited objective programs. In fiscal year 1962, for example, $54 million of economic aid was used for explicit base-rental payments to Morocco, Libya, and Spain. In the past four years, $30 million in economic aid has gone to Trinidad-Tobago in return for Navy base rights at Trinidad. [8] However, as of early 1967, A.I.D. no longer has and is unlikely to resume responsibility for financing explicit base rental in any country. The base in Morocco has been shut down. The agreement with Trinidad-Tobago was completed as of July 1967.

---

[6] A.I.D., *Proposed Economic Assistance Program,* FY 1967, p. 125.

[7] *New York Times,* April 29, 1967.

[8] A.I.D., *op. cit.,* p. 96.

The Department of Defense has assumed responsibility for bases in Spain and Libya. There remain a few programs, such as those in Panama and Ethiopia, which are without question larger than they would be in the absence of U.S. strategic facilities in the countries, but where the content of the programs is substantially developmental.

Finally, in the past five years there have been several small "holding action" programs conducted in countries where the current regime was so anti-Western or so difficult to work with that the United States sought merely to preserve some ties with friendly groups in the population or to avoid the total collapse of diplomatic relations that would probably result from terminating aid. As one journalist put it, describing the program in Ben Bella's Algeria, "In present circumstances there is very little the U.S. can do . . . except hang on, try to clear up misunderstandings where possible, and keep the flag flying." [9] Holding action programs were conducted in Ghana under Nkrumah, in British Guinea under Jagan, and in Indonesia during the last year or so of Sukarno's control, as well as in Algeria. In Haiti, as noted earlier, U.S. disapproval is so strong that aid has been withheld since 1963 except for the malaria eradication work conducted largely through international organizations.

All types of limited objective programs taken together—presence programs in sub-Saharan Africa, token programs in several Latin American countries, counter-Communist programs, and holding actions—account for close to half the total number of A.I.D. country assistance programs. But during the last few years they have absorbed a small and falling fraction of total A.I.D. assistance—2 per cent in 1966.

The limited objective programs have recently included only one country—Indonesia—which is clearly of great importance to U.S. policy and where aid can be expected to become large as Indonesia's new regime directs attention to internal growth and takes needed reform measures. [10] Ghana and Algeria also have good growth prospects and play active roles in regional affairs; under current, more responsible regimes, U.S. assistance may increase. With these and possibly one or two other exceptions, the limited objective programs are likely to remain limited, that is, they will not be transformed into more extensive efforts. In other words, since limited objective programs are not

9 Robert Estabrook, *Washington Post,* June 8, 1965.

10 In early January 1967, Administration officials announced that they were prepared in principle to underwrite Indonesian economic stabilization by providing as much as $80 million during the year (*New York Times,* January 7, 1967).

change-oriented, they do not have an evolving "life-cycle" like that described for security and development programs.

On the other hand, while development-oriented programs are designed to work themselves out of existence eventually, there are no readily defined criteria for terminating limited objective programs. Theoretically such programs could continue until aid no longer effectively served the primary U.S. interest, perhaps because the country had progressed (with more substantial aid from other donors) to the point where it no longer needed external assistance.

To summarize, in the five-year period from 1962 through 1966, a little over 30 country programs, accounting for two thirds of total A.I.D. country program funds, focused primarily on promoting long-term economic and social progress. Another seven or eight large programs were designed to restore security or maintain stability: through 1965, these accounted for a bit over a fifth of total A.I.D. commitments, but in 1966 increased expenditures in Vietnam raised the proportion to two fifths. Finally, limited objective programs were conducted in 35 or 40 countries, but accounted for roughly 6 per cent of total outlay during the entire five years and for only 2 per cent by the final year of the period. The number of countries in each category changes from year to year, because the nature of some programs changes, and because some programs are terminated and others are begun or resumed after being temporarily discontinued. Within each group, moreover, different programs show substantial differences, often reflecting the relative strength of secondary program objectives. The categories help to make sense out of an otherwise bewildering array of disparate efforts, but fall well short of accounting for the precise design of individual country programs.

Is U.S. Economic Assistance Too Dispersed?

In fiscal 1966, A.I.D. assistance went to 74 countries. To spread aid so thin, it is argued, overstrains our resources and reduces the effectiveness of our assistance in those countries where truly major U.S. interests are at stake.

However, a glance at the distribution of assistance among types of country programs shows that this argument is less persuasive than it may appear at first glance. U.S. economic aid is in fact quite concentrated. Three quarters of developmental aid goes to major development programs in eight countries. Vietnam alone accounts for two thirds of security assistance. Conversely, many countries receive very small amounts of aid. Eliminating all of the limited objective programs would free only 2 per cent of total funds for other uses. Of course, dollars are not the only scarce U.S. resource. Administrative attention in particular is certainly more diffused than dollar outlay. Eliminating many of the smaller programs might improve the quality of administration and analysis in the remaining programs. These gains would have to be weighed against the foreign policy losses incurred by terminating some programs.

It may well be that these losses would not be great. In other words, many of the limited objective programs may serve relatively low-priority U.S. interests, or, alternatively, although the foreign policy goals sought may be important, aid may be an ineffective instrument to secure them. For some years there has been a hot debate as to whether the presence programs in tropical Africa are worth the funds and effort expended on them. The holding action programs have also been sharply criticized as not merely low-priority but actively harmful, in that they give the appearance of U.S. support for regimes of which we disapprove.

In 1966, longstanding Congressional concern over the number of countries receiving aid led to a series of amendments to the basic legislation restricting the number of countries outside Latin America in which different types of funds could be used. Development loan funds were authorized for use in no more than ten countries in fiscal 1968; [11] 20 countries in Asia and Africa had received such loans in fiscal 1966. Technical assistance was to be restricted to 40 countries outside of Latin America. [12] A.I.D. was then providing technical assistance to 49. Supporting assistance (for political and security uses) was to go to at most 13 countries, [13] the number of countries receiving such assistance at the time. The amendments originated in the Senate. The House Foreign Relations Committee opposed the action, arguing that arbitrary limits on the number of countries to which aid could be provided hampered the conduct of foreign policy with compensating gains. The Committee observed:

Cutting aid or limiting the number of countries does not provide either the guidance or the means of redirecting our foreign policy. . . . It is not to our advantage to impose restrictions on the purposes or the countries for which these tools can be used, the effect of which is to deprive us of the means for dealing with situations which may occur.[14]

[11] Foreign Assistance Act of 1966, Section 102(a)(2) amending Section 201(b) of the 1961 Act.

[12] *Ibid.,* Section 103(a)(2) amending Section 211(a) of the 1961 Act.

[13] *Ibid.,* Section 108(a) amending Section 401 of the 1961 Act.

[14] Eighty-ninth Congress, 2nd Session, House Report 1651, June 23, 1966.

The Senate view prevailed in the Conference reconciling differences between the House and Senate versions of the bill.

Regardless of one's views as to the usefulness of the small programs, it seems clear that a legislative limit on the number of countries aided is a rigid and clumsy device addressed to the wrong issue. The question is not whether too many countries receive U.S. aid—a question that makes little sense as stated—but rather whether U.S. funds and administrative resources are so dispersed as to reduce their effectiveness, and whether individual programs or groups of programs yield foreign policy benefits commensurate with their costs. The answer to the first question is that funds are in fact highly concentrated, but that modest gains in administrative and analytic quality might be expected from an aid effort confined to a smaller number of countries. The second question can only be answered by detailed examination of the programs at issue, which is done in Chapter 5.

CHAPTER 3

Program Planning

THE PRECISE AMOUNT and composition of aid to particular countries is largely determined through an elaborate annual program planning process. The process has inherent limitations, which should be stated immediately.

Program analysis takes U.S. foreign policy objectives in each country as given. Therefore, if some U.S. interests conflict with others—for example, desire to press for reforms versus concern for the immediate stability or the good will of the host government—the conflict will be reflected in inconsistent or vacillating aid programs.

The current program also constrains planners. Few technical or capital assistance projects are completed in one year. At any one time, the bulk of most country assistance programs consists of projects started several years earlier and not yet completed. The country situation, or U.S. judgment of priorities, or the nature of the U.S. interest in the country may have changed in the interim. But the projects cannot be abruptly broken off or modified without badly damaging mission morale, violating contractual obligations, and, in all likelihood, straining relations with the aided country.

The annual program analysis is intended as a serious reappraisal of the current program and a framework for future programs. But those who planned the current program are understandably committed to it. If they have been replaced by newcomers, the latters' fresh look is properly constrained by the knowledge that the total program cannot be abruptly or radically altered. Therefore, the major contribution of good program analysis and planning is to guide new activities and additional measures to promote self-help—a fraction of total activity. This is not necessarily unfortunate. Most development measures require sustained effort. Moreover, U.S. economic assistance is afflicted with periodic fads: community development is the key to growth one year; human resource development is the watchword a few years later. It may be better to stick with and accomplish a "second best" program than to disrupt U.S. and host country efforts with repeated changes.

A still more fundamental constraint is our inadequate knowledge about development. The benefits expected from proposed major changes should be great enough to allow for substantial margins of error. And yet, precisely because our knowledge is inadequate, program planning must be flexible enough to accommodate new ideas and approaches. The line between continuity and inertia is often hard to draw.

Finally, many aid decisions are made completely outside the annual planning cycle. This is true of many, though not all, short-run political uses of aid.

These constraints sometimes make the program planning process look like an elaborate play-act, with little connection to actual action. Yet for all its limitations, the annual program cycle remains the single most important channel for decisions regarding U.S. economic aid. It affects some kinds of aid much more directly and immediately than others. The volume of commodity assistance and the self-help conditions attached to such assistance are largely determined by annual analysis. Selection and design of new technical assistance projects is less closely tied to overall analysis, and capital projects float more loosely still, for reasons discussed later in this chapter. In terms of types of country programs, the annual program planning process is much more relevant and important for development programs than for programs that emphasize security or limited political objectives.

Programming Principles

Among the program planning principles that have emerged from twenty years' experience with large-scale foreign aid programs, the most basic are the closely linked concepts of country programming and concentration. Country programming implies both tailoring U.S. efforts to the particular circumstances of the individual country, and coordinating all types of U.S. aid into an integrated "country program" rather than conducting semi-independent technical, capital, and commodity aid efforts. Concentration simply means focusing aid on a few high-priority goals.

Although these concepts long predate the 1961 establishment of the Agency for International Development, earlier administrative structure hindered their application. Before 1961 the International Cooperation Administration (ICA) had been responsible for administering technical assistance, defense support, and "special assistance" (for political and certain security purposes). A separate organization, the Development Loan Fund, managed capital loans, operating as a development bank lending for sound capital projects on easy terms. The fact that separate agencies administered the several forms of U.S. assistance made it difficult to design and administer total U.S. assistance to a country as an integrated program. The resulting pattern of aid was so diffuse that it risked having little impact in any field.

To put the problem slightly differently, it is obvious that a program comprised of poorly designed projects will not achieve its goals. But a program can also be made up of projects that are carefully planned and well-administered, yet fail to address the most important problems, or are too dispersed, or too poorly integrated with each other and with host government efforts to have a significant impact.

The 1961 merger of the International Cooperation Administration and the Development Loan Fund was intended to facilitate a unified aid effort. President Kennedy appointed a Task Force on Foreign Economic Assistance to draw up guidelines for the new agency and program. The Task Force Report noted that "our efforts to stimulate economic development in the past have suffered from a piecemeal approach." Moreover, poor development planning in many of the developing countries themselves "has been condoned if not fostered by our own project-by-project approach to foreign assistance." [1] Therefore, the Task Force urged that future programs in each country be based on a comprehensive analysis of needs and capabilities and on selection of a few key goals on which to concentrate U.S. assistance.

It is common sense to concentrate limited resources (not only dollars, but also limited numbers of qualified U.S. specialists who are willing to serve abroad under often trying circumstances) where they will do the most good. Moreover, as the Task Force Report implied, concentrating aid is important for best use of the host country's scarce resources as well as the donor's. Each project that is partially supported by foreign assistance also absorbs host country resources. Capital projects call for labor and locally available materials. Technical assistance requires host country officials or technicians to work with the foreign advisors. Usually it also involves office space, local transportation, and supplies. Moreover, reaching agreement on and implementing any sizeable project usually demands the time and attention of the painfully thin layer of top-level host country administrative and professional officials—perhaps the scarcest resource of all. Therefore, there is both a double motivation and a double responsibility to concentrate assistance on priority tasks.

Stated abstractly, these principles sound obvious and innocuous. Applied, they become more controversial. For example, most develop-

---

[1] President's Task Force on Foreign Economic Assistance, "The Act for International Development: A Program for the Decade of Development," 1961, p. 9.

ing countries suffer appalling rates of disease, malnutrition, and infant mortality. Yet, in some, direct measures to improve health may warrant far less attention than increased productivity in agriculture, which will contribute rapidly and directly to higher incomes and thus indirectly to improved health. Therefore, it might be concluded that little or no assistance should be given to some countries in the field of health. The decision to exclude health (or adult literacy, or community development, or any of many other fields) is likely to raise protests within and outside A.I.D. Evidence of what will contribute most to rapid growth is seldom clear-cut. Specialists in every field can point to the myriad connections between improvements in health (or labor relations, or police competence) and rapid growth. Indeed, each specialist is likely to believe that his field is the key to across-the-board development. Particularly if a country has already been receiving aid in a particular field, perhaps for some time, terminating aid in that field may cause protest from the recipient government and almost certainly will be resisted by the relevant A.I.D. specialists in the mission and in Washington.

Other parts of the U.S. Government or private U.S. organizations may press for more action in particular fields, inadvertently encouraging diffusion. For example, organized labor strongly urges A.I.D. action (and itself provides both personnel and additional funds) to assist development of labor unions abroad. Congress has repeatedly stressed the need to build up private enterprise in the developing countries and has also indicated special favor for cooperatives, community development, and local government as instruments of economic growth and democratic evolution. In autumn 1965, President Johnson announced a program of bold "new initiatives" in the fields of agriculture, education, and health, involving A.I.D., other U.S. Government agencies, and the cooperation of U.S. universities and other private organizations.

If special concerns are permitted to force the introduction of particular kinds of activity into each country program, regardless of Embassy and A.I.D. judgment regarding priorities in the individual country setting, the basic principles of country programming and concentration can be impaired. For example, in 1962 and 1963, an interdepartmental committee's concern over internal security problems led to a sharp increase in funds for police training and the introduction of such programs in a number of countries where A.I.D. program criteria would not have given them high priority.

On the other hand, external pressures undoubtedly push A.I.D. to re-examine its own priorities and approaches. A.I.D., like all organizations, tends to ossify. Statements by the President or Congress emphasizing particular fields may also refresh public interest and support for foreign aid. President Johnson's "three initiatives" are undoubtedly simpler, more concrete, and more appealing than the elusive concept of individual programs tailored to each country's needs.

Self-help is a third major program planning principle. The developing countries' own broad policies—reasonable control of inflation, the pattern and administration of import controls, incentives for foreign and domestic private investment, the efficiency and honesty of administration in general—profoundly affect the productivity of all inputs, external and domestic. Therefore, once assistance goals have been selected for a particular country, it is as important to identify the key self-help measures which must be taken as to assess what capital and technical aid may be needed. Nor does the task stop with identifying crucial host government action. Devising means to encourage that action is an essential aspect of program planning.

In principle, identifying and encouraging major reforms are important in both development and security programs—perhaps even more important in the latter. In practice, it is hard to insist on difficult self-help measures from fragile and already hard-pressed governments. In limited objective programs, the principle is less applicable both in theory and in practice. Most limited objective programs are too small to permit effective influence on important self-help measures. Moreover, efforts to exercise such influence might jeopardize the main objectives of the aid. However, when a program shifts from emphasis on security or on a limited objective such as countering foreign Communist influence to more developmental goals, emphasis on self-help increases accordingly, as occurred in Korea and Afghanistan.

A fourth major programming principle is long-run planning, that is, planning that tries to anticipate trends and problems and to set appropriate targets for several years into the future, rather than considering only the coming budget year. Significant changes can rarely be accomplished in a year or fifteen months. Longer-run planning permits improved coordination and phasing of complementary projects, and advance identification of and efforts to avoid bottlenecks. For example, requirements for sizeable numbers of people with certain skills must be anticipated long in advance, since general education plus specialized training may take ten or fifteen years. A horizon of several years may also change one's views of relative priorities. Projects or targets that look questionable in the short run may appear much more promising or even imperative in the context of changes expected in the next five years. A.I.D. has pressed the developing countries to formulate long-term national plans to permit coordinated progress toward realistic targets. The same principle applies to A.I.D. itself.

But anticipating trends is no simple matter. Data in developing countries are notoriously poor. Factors such as politics, weather, or world prices for key exports may have a profound impact on economic progress, but they cannot be predicted. These problems affect both host country and A.I.D. planning. A.I.D. has the additional problem of anticipating the course of relations between the aided country and the United States. Therefore, A.I.D.'s efforts to conduct long-run analysis and planning have been concentrated in those countries where data are comparatively good and both internal political structure and relations with the United States seem reasonably stable. These are the major development programs. In countries where the United States conducts security and stability programs, the situation is normally too unpredictable to permit planning more than a year in advance; indeed, plans are often revised several times in the course of a year to adjust to rapidly changing circumstances. In limited objective programs, the restricted nature of U.S. goals makes long-run planning efforts unnecessary. Ideally, however, in most programs primarily directed to development, A.I.D. goals should be stated in terms of changes to be brought about through joint host country, U.S., and other donor efforts over a period of several years.

Even though its application has been limited to the larger development programs, the principle of long-run planning is less well accepted within A.I.D. than the principles of country programming, concentration, and self-help, perhaps in part because its application calls for analytic skills that most A.I.D. personnel lack. Still more controversial within A.I.D. is a fifth principle, that of formally exploring several alternative courses of action and spelling out the pros and cons of each before settling on the preferred program. Much of the pressure for this approach has come from the Bureau of the Budget, which often requires A.I.D. to lay out the implications of alternative levels of total assistance before recommending that the President request a particular amount from Congress. These requirements were formalized and broadened in autumn 1965, when the Bureau announced that almost all Executive Branch departments and agencies, including A.I.D., were to adopt a new "Planning-Programming-Budgeting System" (PPBS) based on principles developed in the Department of Defense. A.I.D. was already applying many of the PPBS principles—establishment of a permanent programming staff, derivation of program and budget proposals from broad objectives and priority goals rather than extrapolation of current activities, anticipation of not only the budget-year costs of proposed action but also the continuing costs in later years. However, the system also laid great stress on thorough and explicit analysis of alternatives. Although not a new idea to A.I.D., this certainly was not being carried out in practice.

This does not mean that alternatives are not considered at every stage of program formulation and review. In field missions, program officers make themselves unpopular with technical division heads by sharply questioning the need for proposed activities and by insisting on consideration of possible alternatives. Mission Directors do the same. Embassies may often press for a higher level of aid than A.I.D. staff believe is realistic to request, or urge greater priority for activities that may reduce political unrest, or suggest other modifications. A similar process goes on during Washington review of field proposals. If the field mission has recommended providing commodity assistance, review sessions probe into the consequences of providing less than the mission proposed. (Occasionally reviewers also consider whether growth might be substantially accelerated by providing *more* commodity aid than the field mission proposed.) The choice of fields of concentration and self-help conditions are also examined. But this consideration of alternatives is seldom backed up by a systematic comparison of the costs and benefits of each course under consideration.

Lack of formal and systematic analysis of alternatives is partly due simply to limited staff time. It is often as much as the field mission can manage (along with its other responsibilities) to set forth a well-reasoned and documented annual case for a single course of action, without also developing the arguments for and against various alternatives. Moreover, at each level, once review has been completed, the reviewers become advocates of their conclusions. Thus, if a mission sets forth alternatives for Washington to examine, they are likely to be straw men intended primarily to demonstrate the validity of the course endorsed by the mission. Similarly, A.I.D. is an advocate of its programs vis-à-vis the Bureau of the Budget. Still a third factor is the widespread feeling in A.I.D. that programs are already overreviewed. Officials in field missions and Washington find it exasperating to explain repeatedly the rationale for continuing lines of action, which were justified last year and the year before that. (A common A.I.D. complaint: "They are always pulling up the plant and looking at its roots to see why it doesn't grow.") All this adds up to considerable resistance to formal and extensive analysis of alternatives.

The Programming Process

The principles just outlined are applied within an elaborate annual program planning cycle. The cycle begins with instructions from A.I.D. offices in Washington to the field missions,[2] calling for each mission's analysis of the host country situation and its program proposals for the coming budget year. In assessing the host country situation and drawing up recommendations as to the volume and content of economic assistance, a mission consults with the U.S. Embassy and with other interested U.S. agencies working in the country, including the Peace Corps and the Military Assistance Group. The Ambassador approves the submission before it is sent to Washington.

In Washington, the field submissions are examined at several levels, culminating in the A.I.D. Administrator's review of each major program. Mission directors and their program officers are usually called to Washington to participate in these reviews. Representatives of the Departments of State, Defense, Agriculture (with respect to Food for Peace), and of the Treasury and other agencies also attend the reviews to the extent that their responsibilities are involved. Although the field mission contributes an intimate and up-to-date knowledge of country circumstances and the current program, Washington staff are often more objective, have a more balanced sense of priorities among countries in view of probable budget constraints, and perhaps are more sensitive to possible effects of proposed actions in third countries. Washington staff can also contribute experience from other countries in coping with similar problems. Specific questions or suggestions raised in the reviews are usually referred back to the missions, so that the reviews are part of a continuing dialogue between the field and Washington.

After the field submissions have been sharpened to the satisfaction of A.I.D. in Washington, working in consultation with other inter-

---

[2] A.I.D. maintains field missions in all countries to which it extends aid, except for some of the sub-Saharan African nations where aid is limited to small "presence" programs. Larger missions, like those in India or Brazil, may number over 200 Americans, primarily technical assistance specialists and advisors plus a few economic analysts and some administrative personnel. The A.I.D. mission director, like the head of the U.S. Information Service, the Peace Corps representative, and the chief of the Military Assistance Group (if there is one), is responsible directly to the U.S. Ambassador. But the A.I.D. mission is usually a separate establishment with its own offices, and A.I.D. personnel often substantially outnumber Embassy staff.

ested agencies, the proposed worldwide program, including some seventy country programs plus regional and other noncountry activities, is submitted to the Bureau of the Budget. The Bureau subjects the proposals to further review, focusing on larger programs in general and on any specific proposals which involve unusually large sums of money or politically delicate or important judgments. Some of these may be called to White House attention.

Once the proposed worldwide program has been approved by the executive branch, it is submitted to Congress with a request for authorization and appropriation of the necessary funds. Congress does not approve the volume or content of individual country programs, but votes on the amount of money appropriated for each of several funding categories used to finance different types of activities, such as, Development Loans, Development Grants and Technical Assistance, Supporting Assistance (for security and political uses), and a Contingency Fund (to meet requirements arising during the year which could not be foreseen, or for which costs could not be estimated when the appropriations request was submitted to Congress). Funds for development loans and technical assistance grants for Latin American countries are voted on as separate funding categories. Therefore Congress can indicate its views on the relative priority of Latin America by the extent to which it cuts Alliance for Progress funds as compared with funds for Africa and Asia.

Although Congress does not vote on each country program, Congressional committees attempt to influence A.I.D. policy toward specific countries through committee reports and by their line of questioning when A.I.D. officials testify in committee hearings. Occasionally, particularly strong feelings about specific country programs appear as restrictions written into the legislation. For example, Congress has repeatedly amended the annual Foreign Assistance Acts to prohibit aid to the UAR and to Indonesia under Sukarno's control. However, such amendments usually provide an "escape clause," that gives the President discretion to continue the program if he finds that this step is in the national interest. On rare occasions Congress has even acted with respect to a specific project. For example, the 1963 Appropriations Act included a clause stating that no funds appropriated could be used for any project costing over $100 million [3] —an effective veto on proposed U.S. assistance for the huge publicly owned Bokaro steel mill in India. But for the most

[3] Foreign Assistance Act of 1963, Section 301(e)(3), adding a new Section 620(k) to the 1961 Act.

part, Congress exerts its influence by writing general policy guidance into the Acts and voting on the level of appropriations for each funding category.

The entire process, from field missions' preparation of the proposed country programs to Congressional approval of authorization and appropriations bills for the worldwide program, takes about 15 months. In other words, missions are asked in spring 1967 to start drawing up program proposals for fiscal year 1969, which runs from July 1, 1968, to June 30, 1969. Field mission analysis requires several months. Review in the Executive Branch in Washington takes at least four months, normally from September through December. Congressional passage of the authorization and appropriation bills may take as long as nine months. The authorization bill is introduced in early spring, but approval of the money bill usually comes only in late summer or early autumn, after the start of the fiscal year for which the funds are needed. Only then can each field mission be informed how much money will be available for its programs during the remainder of the fiscal year, so that it can make a final selection from among proposed projects and negotiate agreements with the host government.

Of course, planning for a period beginning 15 months hence must be tentative, and plans must be modified if conditions change —as they often do. Therefore, the "in-cycle" planning and review process described above is supplemented by an ad hoc process to deal with crises or changed situations as they arise.

What role does the host government play in the programming process? Normally, all proposals for aid originate with the host government. In practice, the specific form and design of individual requests are often worked out jointly by host government and mission staff. But the final decision to request aid in a particular amount and form always rests with the host government.

On the other hand, the mission is responsible for the analysis and strategy recommendations which will largely determine the amount and composition of assistance the United States is willing to extend. In conducting analysis and formulating strategy, the mission takes into account host country plans, policies, and attitudes. If there is a national development plan that the mission judges to be broadly sound, mission recommendations will be designed to fit in with and support the plan. Aid officials view as part of their job the continuing exchange of views with host country personnel. An A.I.D. program officer or economic advisor is expected to establish contacts with officials in the Ministry of Finance, the national planning organization, and the central statistical organization or its equivalent, and with host country businessmen, bankers, economists, and other individuals who are knowledgeable about the economy as a whole or whose views are influential. Similarly, an A.I.D. agriculture division chief contacts Ministry of Agriculture officials, leaders of cooperative and credit organizations, and staff members of agricultural faculties at host country universities. Ideally, there is a year-round exchange of information and ideas on trends, the nature of problems impeding progress, the pros and cons of possible host country policies and programs, and what the U.S. might do to help. This ideal is only partially realized, but A.I.D. officials normally bring to the programming process a fairly thorough knowledge of host government attitudes. Their contacts outside official circles are generally more limited, which may be a serious shortcoming in countries where official and popular attitudes diverge.

However, early discussions regarding the volume and content of aid the United States will be prepared to provide to a particular country during the coming year are usually conducted privately within the U.S. Government. There may be some degree of informal consultation with the host government even at this stage, but several considerations limit the extent of such consultation. A principal constraint is that field proposals are likely to be interpreted as in some sense commitments. A great deal can happen between the time a field program is submitted and aid is committed. Washington may disagree with the judgments of the mission and Embassy as to what should be done. Washington and the field may agree but Congressional cuts in total appropriations may force drastic revision of some country programs. The situation in the country or the nature of U.S. interests in that country or in others may change, altering previous judgments on aid priorities. Therefore, discussion of tentative U.S. plans with the host government far in advance of readiness to make firm commitments is risky.

To the extent that U.S. goals or means are not identical with those of the host country, prior consultation with the host government is further inhibited. The United States may want to promote development in a particular country where the ruling elite has much less interest in significant change than does the United States. Or the United States may feel that specific controversial reforms are essential to effective growth or stabilization, whereas the host government may disagree. Under such circumstances mission and Embassy proposals must suggest how to encourage the reforms, and ideas regarding tactics normally would not be discussed at this stage with the recipient government.

However, where U.S. and host country objectives coincide, there are great advantages in discussing aid plans with the recipient government from the outset. For example, in Taiwan in the early 1960's, and more recently in Turkey and Korea, the United States and the host governments agreed that termination of U.S. economic aid would be possible within a few years, and proceeded to discuss the timing and manner of aid withdrawal. Such advance consultation permits the host government to adjust its own policies and programs to smooth and speed the transition to self-sustaining growth.

The Content of Program Analysis

This sketch of the program planning process has identified the major steps and actors, but gives little sense of its substance. In theory, program analysis moves through a logical sequence covering the following steps:

1. Identifying the major U.S. objectives that aid is intended to promote in the country.
2. Assessing the host country situation and trends, including its plans, programs, and policies, in order to identify major problems and important lines of potential progress.
3. Anticipating the probable role of other donors during the planning period under consideration.
4. In view of these considerations, selecting more specific goals on which to focus U.S. economic aid. The principle of concentration suggests that these goals be relatively few—say four to six—in number.
5. For each goal, identifying all of the important measures needed, including policy or administrative changes as well as capital investment and creation or improvement of skills and institutions. Many of the necessary actions can be taken only by the host government. The United States may be able to encourage such self-help measures. Other donors may already be assisting with some aspects of the problem, or might be encouraged to do so. Finally, some of the needed measures will be appropriate for direct U.S. action—technical assistance, capital projects or commodity assistance. Very few significant goals can be accomplished solely or primarily through U.S. aid. Therefore, it is important that aid be

viewed in the broader context of all the important measures the goal implies.

Actual programming falls considerably short of the ideal. Some of the links in the chain are much stronger than others.

The statement of U.S. objectives—the logical starting point of program analysis—is almost always a pro forma quotation from earlier submissions or from State Department documents on U.S. policy toward a country. The statement sets a general tone—overriding concern for security and stability, or strong emphasis on development, or perhaps identification of some special U.S. interest. It reflects the current consensus within the U.S. Government regarding policy toward the country. It is seldom an independent or fresh statement of policy. This is as one would expect. The A.I.D. programming process is not the appropriate channel through which to determine basic U.S. policy toward a country. However, as noted earlier, where elements of U.S. policy conflict, the inconsistencies are reflected in the assistance program. This is, of course, a problem of U.S. foreign policy formulation, and only secondarily a problem of A.I.D. programming.

Much fuller and more serious effort goes into the annual assessment of the country situation. For larger programs, particularly for the eight or nine largest development programs, missions may submit studies of several hundred pages, focused primarily on economic questions. The analysis covers recent trends, future prospects, and host government plans and policies regarding public and private investment, savings, consumption, government revenues and expenditures, exports, imports, and the balance of payments, foreign debt; prices, and population growth. In addition, the submission may survey the progress and outlook for major sectors—agriculture, manufacturing, mining, education, and so forth. Missions responsible for smaller programs cut scope somewhat and reduce depth considerably. The size of the missions would not permit such ambitious analysis, nor would the programs warrant it.

The overall economic analysis generally serves three purposes. Especially where aid includes substantial commodity assistance, analysis of the balance of payments and internal monetary and fiscal trends helps to determine the volume of assistance. In general, missions responsible for programs where commodity aid bulks largest do the most thorough overall economic analysis.

Such analysis also helps identify self-help requirements. In estimating progress over, say, a five-year period, field missions do not regard existing host government policies, priorities, and administrative capacity as immutable, but rather as critical variables. On the other hand, clearly the mission does not want to assume radical, therefore highly unlikely, changes in policies, priorities, or efficiency. Much of the purpose of the analysis is, in fact, to pick out those key changes that are both necessary to realize potential growth and feasible in light of major constraints, including political pressures on the host government and competing claims on limited capital and administrative skills.

Finally, in principle overall analysis provides a framework for more intensive sector and project analysis. In practice, for reasons to be discussed, analysis of sectors is often poor, and individual capital and technical assistance projects are selected and designed on grounds only vaguely related to overall analysis.

Assessment of the social and political trends and problems in the country usually is much briefer and more superficial than the economic analysis. It is common practice to request the Embassy political section to prepare this part of the annual submission. The resulting analysis is seldom well integrated into the remainder of the submission. Therefore, proposals for direct efforts by A.I.D. to accelerate social progress and political development rarely rest on systematic and reasonably comprehensive analysis of the problems they address. Such efforts tend to be scattered, uncoordinated with each other, or with more strictly economic aspects of the aid program. Often they are undertaken hastily, to cope with an immediate crisis. Worse, no serious effort is made to assess and thereby guide the social and political effects of the aid effort as a whole.

Although missions try to take into account other donors' plans, these are hard to ascertain. Most other donors do not maintain permanent field staffs in the countries they assist. Occasionally missions ask the U.S. embassies in London, Paris, and Bonn to inquire regarding their plans. But normally the other donors themselves have not determined the volume and content of their assistance to specific countries, and might be reluctant to pass on such information even if it were available. Therefore, A.I.D. missions can do little more than note that particular donors have indicated interest in specific major projects, which are almost ready for funding or are in process of negotiation. Where the major donors are members of formal consortia or consultative groups,[4] better information on others' plans may come out of consultation and pledging sessions.

The statement of U.S. objectives, assessment of the country situation, and expected role of other donors provide a framework within which to select perhaps half a dozen goals on which to concentrate U.S. economic assistance. In selecting goals, missions are also asked to take into account the particular areas of strength and weakness in U.S. assistance. In some fields the United States can offer particularly well-developed techniques, equipment, or institutional experience (agricultural extension, road-building equipment). In other fields (for example, family planning, tourism) other advanced countries may be better qualified to extend assistance. Aside from technical competence, relative prices must be kept in mind. Since U.S. assistance must, with rare exceptions, be used to purchase U.S. goods and services, the United States should seek areas of assistance where it can provide the required skills and commodities at competitive or better-than-competitive prices and qualities. To do otherwise is to depreciate the value of aid.[5]

Goals vary widely. Some cut across production sectors and are closely related to broad economic policies; others coincide with sectors or subsectors. Some are essentially qualitative; others lend themselves to meaningful quantification. Fairly typical goals might include:

—Reorienting the formal education system to better serve manpower and other development needs.

—Increasing agricultural productivity, particularly in export crops.

—Integrating an isolated and dissident region into the nation.

---

[4] Consortia and consultative groups are composed of representatives of the governments and international organizations aiding particular countries. A consortium is pledged to provide a volume of assistance adequate to cover requirements agreed between the recipient and the donors. A consultative group is more informal and is not committed to any specific aid level, but provides a forum in which the recipient may present its case and donors may coordinate their views.

[5] The Treasury and the Department of Commerce have urged that in addition to tying aid to U.S. sources of procurement, A.I.D. insist that imports from the United States purchased with A.I.D. dollars be *additional* to the normal value of the recipient nation's self-financed imports from the United States. Aside from the fact that the "normal level" of imports is difficult to ascertain, particularly where a country has received substantial U.S. aid for a long time, enforcing "additionality" would probably force many countries to purchase goods from the United States that they could buy more cheaply elsewhere. This would help the U.S. balance of payments, but would undercut the purpose of the aid.

—Doubling export earnings by 1972.

—Increasing the proportion of host government expenditures covered by internal revenues to 90 per cent by 1972.

Each of these goals calls for host country action as well as U.S. (and perhaps other donors') aid. Missions are asked to prepare a detailed analysis of each goal, as a basis for selecting specific U.S. activities and focusing U.S. influence on key self-help measures. Take, for example, the goal of reorienting the formal education system to better serve developmental needs. In many developing countries, graduates from high schools and colleges who have majored in arts, social science, or law have trouble finding employment, whereas there is an acute shortage of scientific and technical personnel. In such circumstances, one subgoal might be a shift in the distribution of students at secondary and higher levels from generalist to technical and professional fields of study. Often poor mathematics and science preparation in the early secondary school years impedes such a shift, because students do not feel prepared to pass entrance examinations for science courses. In that case assistance and influence might be focused on substantially increasing the number of qualified mathematics and science teachers at the early secondary level. The host government might also be urged to offer generous scholarships for important but unpopular fields of technical study such as agricultural engineering. Another subgoal might be the introduction, over several years, of terminal technical and commercial programs at secondary and subuniversity level. This subgoal too would call for host government action as well as aid.

At its best, analysis along these lines permits a concentration of U.S. aid on clearly defined targets, according to an integrated goal plan. But the concept of a sharply focused, closely integrated goal plan is seldom realized in practice.

The selection of most goals and the structure of U.S. efforts within each goal depends much more on the pattern of past U.S. assistance in the country and much less on systematic analysis than programming theory would suggest. As noted earlier, the bulk of virtually every country program consists of activities already under way (except in those rare instances when a program is being rapidly expanded, as is currently the case in Ghana). The mission cannot start de novo each year and determine where to concentrate U.S. assistance. Therefore, there is a strong tendency to "package" existing activities in a particular field—education, agriculture, industry—

under labels such as "development of human resources," or "rural development," in order to comply with Washington's directive. The projects may be well- or ill-planned individually and as a group, but superficial packaging adds nothing to their effectiveness. A serious assessment of the rationale for projects in a particular field or for an entire program is most likely to result from the arrival of a particularly capable and aggressive new technical division chief or Mission Director.

Quite apart from the inertia of the ongoing program, the principle that all or almost all activities should be geared to major program goals is particularly hard to apply to capital project loans. It takes a long time to develop a loan proposal to the point where it satisfies technical and economic criteria. In most countries only a handful of capital projects are ready for financing at any given time. A.I.D. has increased assistance for surveys and engineering studies to identify and prepare sound projects for financing, but this has not substantially increased the flow of good project proposals. Therefore, in many countries A.I.D. is likely to finance a capital project which looks economically and technically sound and for which funds on suitable terms are not available from other sources, even if the project has little or no relation to the goal structure of the rest of the U.S. assistance program in the country. As a result, six years after the Development Loan Fund has been incorporated into the rest of the U.S. economic assistance effort, capital project assistance remains poorly integrated with other A.I.D. activities.

Up to 1967, it has also been difficult to integrate Food for Peace commodities and the potential influence generated by food programs with the rest of the assistance effort. This was true in part because jurisdiction was divided between A.I.D. and the Department of Agriculture. Probably more important, until 1967 the surplus disposal and relief motivations have outweighed the development motivation in guiding the program's administration. New Food for Peace legislation in autumn 1966 stresses the need to link food programs with self-help efforts, and should permit closer coordination between this and other forms of economic aid.

Still a fourth factor interferes with formulation of well-integrated goal plans. Despite its many technical specialists, A.I.D. analyzes problems relevant to specific goal plans less well than more general economic and financial problems. Usually goal plan analysis must cut across the boundaries of standard technical specializations, of host country administrative structure, and of A.I.D. mission organization.

For example, the problem of increasing the supply of skills and trainable manpower cannot be approached adequately by examining the formal education system alone. The possibilities of expanding in-service training in industry, modernizing traditional apprenticeship systems in certain trades, and using the army as a school for literacy and for civilian skills such as auto repair must also be taken into account. Nor does a survey of the full range of potential sources of skills training complete the picture. The forces influencing utilization of manpower must also be considered. These include wage structure, private and public labor policies, recruitment to different occupations, and a host of other factors. Even extremely competent and experienced specialists in the administration of school systems, curriculum design, or technical education cannot be expected to cope with this range of considerations. Nor are most manpower or labor specialists sufficiently versatile to do the job. There are at best a handful of men in the entire A.I.D. staff, worldwide, who have the training and experience to analyze systematically the problems of skill creation and utilization, as distinct from improvement of a formal education system.

Similarly, agriculture divisions are staffed with experts in agricultural extension, credit, cooperatives, soils, irrigation and water management, and poultry production. Yet problems of rural development clearly extend into education, transport, pricing policies, taxation, and local government, to name only a few factors.

A.I.D. lacks such expertise partly because it is almost impossible to recruit. The broad-gauged agricultural economist, education planner, or health analyst is everywhere in short supply and great demand. Moreover, in some fields such as education planning, the techniques and concepts of analysis are only now becoming the focus of widespread research and theoretical consideration.

Nor can the problem be adequately solved by bringing in high-level consultants to do a one-time study of a sector. Such studies are rapidly outdated. Moreover, any good study raises as many questions as it answers. Just as the changing overall economic situation needs year-round analysis, so the major areas or sectors on which A.I.D. concentrates its efforts in any particular country demand continuing analysis. Until at least the larger missions can be staffed with adequate analysts for major sectors or goals, most project activity will relate tenuously if at all to the overall economic and social analysis, which is the centerpiece of the mission's annual submission.

Scope and Limits of the Programming Process

Most A.I.D. assistance finds its way to specific uses through the programming process described here. But many individual aid actions result from ad hoc responses to crises and opportunities. In particular, aid for many of the political objectives surveyed in Chapter 1 is often unprogrammed—in other words, it is not decided on as part of the annual process of determining the volume and content of the aid program for the coming year. Aid to respond to an unanticipated crisis, or a crisis the timing of which could not be predicted, is obviously unprogrammed—for example, one-time budget support to stave off a government's collapse, the withholding of aid to indicate disapproval of a military coup and encourage scheduling of elections, suspension of aid because a nation has expropriated U.S. property, reduction of aid to discourage an aggressive foreign policy. Disaster relief, of course, is not preplanned. Similarly, the Mission Director uses his Director's Fund as opportunities appear, although the Fund itself is programmed as part of the country budget for the year.

Some A.I.D. activities are conducted on a regional or world-wide basis, rather than as bilateral aid to individual countries. Such aid is programmed in advance but falls outside the scope of the country programming process discussed in this chapter. Examples include contributions to international organizations, regional programs such as the measles control effort in West Africa, and ocean transport of clothing and other goods donated by U.S. charitable organizations.

Country programs do, however, account for most A.I.D. assistance. And the principles and analysis described apply to all types of country programs, although they are most closely followed for development programs. It is the nature of a security or stability program that there will be more surprises, more crises, more need to alter planned programs and perhaps to draw on the Contingency Fund. Similarly, in counter-bloc and presence programs, economic and technical analysis is less important and political assessment more important than in development programs.

The basic outlines of the program planning process are much like those of any large, complex organization with field offices that deal with widely varying local situations. Many of A.I.D.'s programming problems would sound familiar to planning staff in, for instance, the Department of Health, Education and Welfare—multiple and sometimes conflicting program objectives, many of which cannot be neatly quantified; incomplete or inadequate data and analysis; and the necessity of working with local authorities whose cooperation is essential but whose own priorities and values may diverge sharply from those of the agency. However, A.I.D. must work with independent sovereign governments rather than local or state authorities within a common federal framework. Moreover, U.S. economic aid is probably a smaller fraction of most recipient nations' development efforts than is the federal contribution to many state and local programs. Therefore, the relationship between U.S. input and desired output or achievement is more tenuous than in most domestic programs. Because U.S. control is attenuated and the U.S. contribution is marginal, cost-benefit analysis and other standard planning techniques may be less useful for aid programming than for domestic programs. For the same reasons, analysis of the recipients' own programs and policies and efforts to encourage better performance assume far greater importance.

As noted at the outset, the programming process is intended to serve, not to determine, fundamental U.S. policy toward individual countries. Not infrequently program planning bares basic issues. Sometimes these are taken up through regular foreign policy channels; sometimes they are obscured. Many of the problems associated with the use of aid for influencing economic policies, for short-run political purposes, and for shaping long-run political evolution are problems of priorities among foreign policy objectives and the complementarity or conflict among them. At its best, the program process can raise these issues sharply. It cannot resolve them.

Part Two: AID AS INFLUENCE: POTENTIAL AND LIMITS

CHAPTER 4

Using Aid To Improve Development Policies*

THIS CHAPTER concerns one aspect of developmental aid—the use of all three types of economic aid to encourage improved development policies on the part of the recipient government. Although the terms "influence," "leverage," and "conditions" have strong political connotations, and efforts to promote better policies do indeed involve delicate political considerations as well as complex technical judgments, there should be no confusion between persuasion or even "strings" designed to accelerate growth and the short-run political uses of aid discussed in Chapter 5.

For two reasons, aid's "influence potential" may make a much more important contribution in the long run to promoting progress than its resource contribution. First, as noted earlier, total aid from all sources has contributed a fraction—roughly 25 per cent—of total investment in the developing countries in the past few years. The use made of the self-financed 75 per cent is clearly more important in accelerating growth than is the use of aid alone. Second, policies and procedures—import licensing arrangements, investment codes, marketing board pricing policies, power and transportation rate structures, tax provisions, land tenure systems, to name only a few—affect

* This chapter draws on A.I.D. Discussion Paper No. 9, "Promoting Effective Development Policies: A.I.D. Experience in the Developing Countries," by Clarence Gulick and Joan Nelson, September, 1965; and on A.I.D. Discussion Paper No. 12, "Measures to Ensure the Effective Use of Aid," by Joan Nelson and Gustav Ranis, originally prepared for a conference sponsored jointly by the Overseas Development Institute and the Ditchley Foundation, and held in England June 3–6, 1966.

economic development at least as powerfully as the availability of adequate infrastructure, technical skills, and imported raw materials and equipment.

From the beginning of the post-World War II aid program there were cases in which assistance was contingent on broad policy changes on the part of the recipient. Not infrequently project loans were conditioned on specific host country economic or administrative measures going beyond the scope of the individual project. Much technical assistance has been designed to increase the ability of host governments to formulate and execute self-help policies and measures: for example, planning assistance, establishment or reorganization of budget bureaus, or tax reform and tax administration. However, since 1961, A.I.D. has tried to relate aid to performance somewhat more systematically and consistently than did predecessor agencies.

This trend has been noticeable mainly among the development-oriented programs, and particularly among those development programs that include a major commodity assistance component. Although the U.S. may be even more concerned to encourage reform in programs directed to security and stability than in major development programs, the government may be too fragmented or too harried to be able to respond to pressure, or too fragile to survive a major reform effort. In the very small programs, the modest U.S. role rules out significant U.S. influence on self-help measures.

A.I.D.'s early efforts to link aid more actively and explicitly to improved performance were mainly in Latin America, partly because the Charter of Punta del Este provided a mutually agreed framework of objectives. Moreover, although the United States had conducted small technical assistance programs in Latin America for many years, substantial concessional capital aid began in 1961 with the signing of the Act of Bogota and the initiation of the Alliance for Progress. In contrast, large assistance programs in the Near East and Asia had been under way for some years, and it is more difficult to introduce new practices into established relationships than to start off on the new basis. Moreover, several of the older large programs in Asia involved strong U.S. military interests, which made it difficult to link aid primarily to development performance and efforts. As of 1966, however, economic aid is or has been explicitly linked to major and mutually agreed self-help measures not only in the larger Latin American programs but also in Korea, Taiwan, India, Pakistan, Turkey, Jordan, and Tunisia.

Identifying Self-help Requirements

The first prerequisite for the effective use of aid to encourage self-help measures is obvious: the donor must understand the country situation well enough to identify the most important self-help measures needed. Although easy to state, this is difficult to implement. Therefore, the thorough and continuing analysis described in Chapter 3 is essential for effective use of influence.

Self-help measures may apply to specific activities—such as financing the local costs of a dam or factory, or changing Ministry of Education regulations to permit experimentation with new teaching techniques—or to much broader efforts to reform tax structure, alter investment priorities between sectors, modify an entire import control system, or give substantially greater encouragement and freedom to private initiative. This chapter emphasizes broader policy improvements and the ways in which donors can support and encourage such improvements. However, the success of any development effort depends not only on appropriate general policies, but also on innumerable more limited improvements in organization, management, and policies. These improvements can be encouraged and supported by different aid techniques, including many kinds of technical assistance as well as explicit understandings in connection with loans for capital projects.

It is difficult to say what kinds of self-help measures are likely to be crucial, because country circumstances vary so greatly. Often developing countries face severe inflation accompanied by a seriously deteriorating foreign exchange position. In such cases a fairly standard set of measures are prescribed for financial stabilization: restraint of credit and government deficits, certain kinds of exchange rate adjustments, and tax and tariff measures to restore balance. However, as emphasis shifts from stabilization measures to policies and programs to promote development, it is often harder to identify the most appropriate steps for individual countries. A few general aspects of self-help can be stated fairly clearly. A country should:

1. Increase its supply of skilled manpower and strengthen the institutions that play key roles in planning and carrying out development programs.
2. Increase the scale of its development programs.

3. Increase the productivity of its development expenditures.
4. Encourage broader economic participation, including creation of a favorable climate for private enterprise.
5. Increase its own financing of development and reduce reliance on external sources.
6. Increase exports, and economize on imports to the extent compatible with rapid growth.

The relative importance of these targets varies from country to country and from time to time. The specific measures needed to achieve them are almost infinitely varied. The appropriate measures can be identified for a particular country only on the basis of intensive study of its particular circumstances.

These self-help targets relate most directly to economic progress, although they are likely to affect (and be affected by) social and political trends. Because both U.S. objectives and the developing countries' concerns are broader than economic growth, self-help should also include measures more directly related to social and political aspects of development, such as steps designed to:

1. Increase capacity to maintain stability essential for development, with minimal resort to coercion.
2. Improve the distribution of income, services, and opportunities.
3. Improve protection of fundamental civil liberties and the administration of justice.
4. Broaden meaningful political participation, and permit a wider range of nonviolent dissent and criticism.

But what constitutes "self-help" in the social and political realms is much more a matter of values and beliefs, and less determined by technical considerations, than is true of measures essential for economic progress. Some (not all) aspects of social and political progress are also far more difficult to measure objectively. Therefore, the United States and other donors have given less attention to self-help in political than in economic realms.

Techniques of Encouraging Improved Policies

One approach to the promotion of better self-help is to assess performance to date and to reward those countries having a generally good record with generous aid allocations. In theory, this approach, pursued consistently, should not only concentrate aid in those countries that can use it most effectively but also induce other countries to improve their policies to qualify for increased aid. This approach is ex post facto, in the sense that donors adjust the level and content of their aid to past performance.

A donor may go beyond the ex post facto approach and seek actively to influence the current and future development policies of recipient countries, through discussion and persuasion, through offering technical advice or financial support to make specific reforms easier, and possibly through conditions, incentives, or sanctions.

It would be convenient to rely heavily or entirely on the ex post facto approach, if this were adequate to bring about effective self-help measures. More active efforts to influence self-help involve at least two major and independent risks: the danger of being wrong about what was needed to promote growth, and the risk of being charged with intervention. If aid allocations are made simply in accordance with demonstrated performance, the developing country has full responsibility for any actions taken or not taken. The problem of anticipating the effects of specific measures is avoided by waiting until at least partial returns are in. The donor runs the risk of adverse reaction only to an aid allocation smaller than the recipient country had hoped it might receive—a risk that can hardly be avoided under any circumstances.

Unfortunately, U.S. aid is not distributed among countries in such a way as to provide a strong incentive for effective self-help measures. Because aid is used for security and political purposes as well as to promote development, the pattern of U.S. aid allocations does not favor good performers clearly enough to induce them to maintain their efforts, or to encourage other nations to improve on poor past records. (Nor, for the same reasons, do other donors' aid patterns closely reflect differences in self-help effort among aid-receiving nations.) Moreover, specific self-help measures call for decision and action by individual host country officials or agencies. Except for decisions taken at the highest levels regarding broad economic policy, the connection between specific decisions and the possibility of increased aid available in the future to the country as a whole (not necessarily to the agency that must implement the reform) is too tenuous to have much impact.

Furthermore, some of the most important self-help measures require external support at the time they are taken as a precondition for success. For example, a country considering liberalizing a complex system of import controls, in order to give market forces more free play, must anticipate and be in a position to cope with a possible surge of pent-up demand for imports when controls are lifted. If its foreign exchange reserves are low, external support is essential. Thus, U.S. willingness to make a larger part of its total aid available in the form of a program loan, rather than for specific projects, helped Pakistan decide in July 1964 to remove import controls on major industrial commodities and raw materials. The liberalization brought about in part with U.S. support resulted in much fuller use of existing industrial capacity. For self-help measures of this kind, the ex post facto approach is inadequate.

Finally, the ex post facto approach makes no provision for supporting a government that promises to turn over a new leaf. For example, in Brazil in spring 1964 the Branco regime inherited an immense budget deficit and galloping inflation. The new government needed two or three months to draw up a stabilization and development program; without support in the interim, government services would have been paralyzed and the economic crisis deepened.

For all these reasons, during the past few years A.I.D. has tried to develop better means of directly influencing current and future self-help measures, to supplement the policy of allocating aid partly in accord with past performance. Although external influence is no substitute for host country commitment, governments are not monoliths, and the United States and other donors can use a great many formal and informal opportunities to support groups that want to put through needed reforms. Moreover, some (though by no means all) of the developing countries face an acute shortage of analytic skills to assess their own problems. In such countries, the sheer additional analytic capacity made available through A.I.D. staff, World Bank teams, or other external sources is a crucial supplement to the efforts of the handful of well-trained native economists to diagnose their country's problems and prescribe appropriate measures.

The more successful instances in which the United States has actively influenced current policies have been based on long and thorough discussion between U.S. and host country officials, often conducted over a period of years. Such discussions are facilitated by a fairly close match between host government and donor assumptions regarding long-term goals and priorities. Because those countries not pursuing sound policies and programs are often also less advanced in institutional development and analytic capabilities and less secure politically, the groundwork of discussion and consensus tends to be most difficult to create in those countries where it is most needed.

Recognizing, then, that specific efforts to influence policies must rest on mutual respect and a continuing exchange of views, what are the techniques that have been used to encourage self-help measures? Potentially, all forms of aid can be used to exercise influence. Some forms of aid are better suited to influencing macro-economic policies; others relate more readily to sector or subsector policies. Moreover, some forms lend themselves not only to exercise of influence, but also to the narrower concept of leverage. I use the term "leverage" for actions that go beyond influence and persuasion to condition aid, explicitly or implicitly, on specified host country measures. Leverage may be negative or positive: aid may be withheld unless certain conditions are satisfied, or additional aid may be made available if host country performance achieves specified standards. Positive leverage is sometimes called "incentive programming."

Much technical assistance is designed primarily to influence policies and procedures. Technical advice, of course, is intended to influence policies directly. Training programs may indirectly affect policies, by sharpening analytic skills and shaping basic attitudes and assumptions. However, with rare exceptions, technical assistance has been used for *leverage* only to facilitate the operation of the project itself, for instance, refusal to enter into or continue a project unless adequate counterparts are provided or the host country fulfills commitments regarding office space, transportation, or other supporting services. The fact that technical assistance projects are rarely used for leverage on host country actions beyond the scope of the projects themselves reflects the assumption that host governments are not sufficiently eager to get or keep specific technical assistance as to be willing to alter sectoral or subsectoral policies or procedures. Most technical assistance projects are relatively small. Often they reflect the donor's view of what needs to be done more than the host government's priorities. Many recipient countries do not count technical assistance as part of the aid level.

There is another constraint on using technical assistance to exert leverage. Effective technical assistance depends much more directly and heavily than other forms of aid on good relations between the foreign technicians and the organization or officials with whom they work. Pressure for reforms, say, in sectoral or subsectoral policy might require decision or action from the counterpart organization itself. If it did, and if the pressure were resented, the gains from the immediate improvement in policy might be vitiated by reduced long-run effectiveness of the technical assistance itself.

Capital assistance for specific projects can be used to exert both general influence and specific leverage on host country actions. At the simplest level, virtually all donors, bilateral and multilateral, insist that engineering and technical criteria essential to the success of the capital project itself be satisfied. These conditions may go beyond sound design and construction to consider efficient use of the project after it is completed—for instance, provision for proper maintenance. Most donors also call for some host country contribution to local costs. These requirements themselves may have a constructive influence, by educating host country officials in what constitutes a well-planned project. However, such conditions also slow the rate of commitments and disbursements, making it difficult to build up and maintain development momentum. The proper balance between upholding high *standards* of project selection and design, and maintaining or increasing the *volume* of investment depends on individual country circumstances.

A.I.D., the International Bank for Reconstruction and Development (World Bank), and other donors may also attach to aid for capital projects conditions going beyond the individual project to affect the performance of an entire sector or subsector. For example, a sizeable A.I.D. loan for road construction in Afghanistan was conditioned on the Government's establishing, staffing, and budgeting for a national highway maintenance department. Loans for power stations in Korea were conditioned on changes in rate structure designed to encourage more economical use of electricity and to generate funds for increased investment in the power field. A loan to the Bolivian Mining Bank to finance expansion and modernization of the private mining industry was not to be disbursed pending major reform of the country's mining code, a reorganization of the bank itself, and the passage and enforcement of new mineral export tax laws to encourage investment in mining.[1]

Perhaps the most important constraint on the use of capital project aid for leverage is the fact that for many developing countries, the volume of assistance available from all sources for sound and well-designed capital projects substantially exceeds the availability of project proposals that meet these criteria. If for diplomatic reasons, several donors are eager to provide substantial aid to a country, but wish to maintain high development standards, they will compete more or less openly for the most attractive projects. Such competition deters donors from attaching conditions extending beyond the scope of the project. Even if competition is not a factor, donors often are reluctant to strain

[1] A.I.D., *Proposed Economic Assistance Programs,* FY 1967, p. 51.

diplomatic relations with the recipient government by delaying commitment of funds for sound projects.

A.I.D. has thus far found loans for commodity imports the most powerful and flexible means of influencing macro-economic policies, in those countries to which such loans are extended. This is true for several reasons:

1. Loans for commodity imports are almost always larger in volume than individual projects; in a number of countries U.S. program loans substantially exceed total project aid.

2. Most donors are reluctant to finance commodity imports. Yet such aid may be badly needed at certain stages of development, to permit fuller utilization of existing facilities and to support widely scattered small capital improvements, which are difficult to finance on a project basis. Moreover, commodity aid flows quickly; its effects on the economy are prompt. If aid is tied (that is, must be used to purchase donor country products), commodity aid gives the aid-receiving country the option of purchasing those goods which the donor produces cheaply and well, whereas aid for specific projects is much less flexible. Therefore, commodity assistance is strongly desired and has high scarcity value.

3. Because commodity imports provide equipment, raw materials, and spare parts for the economy as a whole, a linking of program loans to broad economic policies is more likely to seem reasonable to the recipient. The volume of program lending is usually based on an analysis of balance of payments requirements. This analysis can easily be broadened into a general review of the economic situation, conducted jointly with the host government, and resulting in decisions regarding both the volume of aid and required self-help actions. Recent program loan agreements with Brazil, Chile, Colombia, and Korea have provided for joint quarterly reviews of the economic situation and of progress on particular problems.

4. Once a donor has agreed to finance a specific project, it cannot normally reduce the promised amount. A dam or plant abandoned half-completed is a waste of resources and a visible reproach to the donor. But commodity aid can be increased or decreased at the margin or delayed in timing. Therefore it provides a credible incentive. Program loan agreements with Brazil, Chile, and Colombia have stipulated that assistance would be released in quarterly slices contingent on host country performance as measured

by agreed indicators. When Colombia delayed difficult but vital decisions regarding its exchange rate and budget during 1965, A.I.D. held up disbursement of program loans and did not negotiate a new loan until late in 1965, when Colombia took the needed measures.[2] As a result, A.I.D. commitments to Colombia dropped from $74 million in fiscal year 1964 to only $3.6 million, consisting entirely of technical assistance, in fiscal year 1965.[3] International lending agencies also cut off aid pending reform.[4] Similarly, in August 1966 the United States agreed to lend Ecuador $10 million in three installments, conditional on Ecuador's undertaking a tax reform program. When Ecuador proved unable to implement fully the agreed reforms, the United States withheld the final installment of $3 million.[5] Conversely, a 1966 agreement with Korea provided $15 million in commodity assistance as an incentive for performance exceeding routine plans. The funds were to be released in two installments. For the first six months, the targets included collection of total domestic revenues greater than $166 million, and the limiting of net domestic credit to less than $218 million. The Koreans met both targets, and A.I.D. released $7.5 million.[6]

5. Commodity aid is particularly effective in encouraging certain kinds of reform such as removal of complex and growth-inhibiting import controls. Such reforms cause immediate increases in demand for imports, which can be met only with external aid not tied to specific projects. Major import liberalization measures in Pakistan in 1964 and in India in 1965 depended heavily on increased U.S. commodity assistance to help cover an anticipated jump in import demand. Measures to stimulate private sector activity may also require program support, because neither improvements in thousands of small private plants nor the raw materials and spare parts needed to utilize capacity more fully can be financed efficiently on a project-by-project basis.

Until 1967, food aid (which is one type of commodity assistance) was not normally linked to development self-help measures. The main

[2] A.I.D., *Proposed Economic Assistance Programs,* FY 1967, p. 53.
[3] *U.S. Overseas Loans and Grants,* July 1, 1945–June 30, 1965, p. 34.
[4] *New York Times,* November 30, 1965.
[5] *New York Times,* April 15, 1967.
[6] Don Oberdorfer, "Korea Moving Closer to Self-Reliance," in *Korean Report,* Vol. VI, No. 3, July–September 1966 (published by the Korean Embassy in Washington).

criteria were need for and ability to use the kinds of commodities in surplus supply in the United States without disrupting normal patterns of commercial imports from the United States and from other agricultural exporters. This pattern reflected the surplus disposal motivation of the original Food for Peace program. However, U.S. stocks of surplus agricultural commodities (except cotton) are now largely exhausted, and the 1966 legislation revamping Public Law 480 states a new policy: that the United States should deliberately use its immense agricultural productivity to produce commodities for grant or sale to the developing countries *as an aspect of foreign aid*. The new legislation also provides that food aid in the future is to be linked with self-help efforts, particularly efforts to increase agricultural production.[7] The precise techniques of linking Food for Peace assistance with self-help remain to be worked out. Experience with program loan negotiations may provide some useful guidance.

Commodity aid, including food aid, often leads to U.S. ownership or partial control of sizeable amounts of host country currencies, thereby providing an additional channel through which to exert influence. When U.S. agricultural commodities are sold to a developing country under the Food for Peace program, the United States often is repaid in the country's own currency. The United States then owns that currency. Moreover, when A.I.D.-financed imports are sold in the recipient country, often some part of the proceeds is set aside in a separate account in the country's Central Bank. The United States does not own this currency, but by agreement with the host government, it may exercise joint control over disposition of the funds.

The United States may use its ownership or control over local currency to influence resource allocation, that is, it may urge or insist that these funds be used to increase investment in particular fields. Or it may use control over local currency to encourage other reforms. In Pakistan, for example, U.S.-owned rupees were used as a lever to encourage increased public savings. Pakistan had begun its Second Five-Year Plan (1960–1965) with a poor record of mobilizing resources through taxation: the tax yield was only 6 per cent of GNP. The new Plan contemplated increased taxation, but by mid-Plan it was clear that the limited steps that had been taken would produce only

[7] Food for Peace Act, 1966, Sections 2, 103-a, and 109.

There is no economic reason why food aid should be linked to agricultural reforms rather than to self-help efforts in any other important field. But many U.S. Congressmen and officials (and, perhaps, some recipient country officials) feel that agricultural progress is a particularly appropriate target of leverage exerted through food aid.

about half the modest planned increase in tax yields. The A.I.D. mission estimated that taxes would have to be increased at least to the level projected in the Plan early in 1964, if other aspects of the Plan were not to be impaired. Before the fourth year of the Plan, the United States urged action to increase taxes and backed up its advice by refusing to release U.S.-owned rupees, which would have allowed Pakistan to finance the fourth-year program without a tax increase. Partly because of this pressure, and perhaps more because of increased Pakistani recognition of the need for greater self-help effort, Pakistan raised additional taxes for the year in an amount greater than 1 per cent of GNP, the largest tax increase in Pakistan's history. Further tax measures were enacted the following year, so that Pakistan ended its Second Plan with tax yields somewhat over 9 per cent of GNP.[8]

Commodity assistance, then, provides a versatile and effective means of influencing recipients' economic policies. Capital assistance permits more limited leverage, and technical assistance may be used to provide advice and analytic expertise in important areas of reform.

Still another device to encourage improved self-help was set forth in the guidelines drawn up in 1961 by the President's Task Force on Foreign Economic Assistance, but has since been virtually abandoned. This approach is the long-term commitment. The Task Force Report stated:

Perhaps the most important incentive for [the developing countries] will be clear evidence that where other countries have done this kind of home work we have responded with longterm commitments. . . . In order that we can be in a position to make the necessary longterm commitments, we are requesting five-year borrowing authority for the Development Loan portion of the overall aid program.[9]

Congress did not approve the request for five-year borrowing authority, but did give the newly created Agency for International Development authority to commit the United States to make available to the recipient country a stated volume of assistance over a period of several years, subject to annual appropriation of funds. Because the sum of such commitments for any year was not expected to exceed a fraction of the worldwide program, annual appropriations would not interfere with exercise of this authority. Long-term commitments were in fact made to India and Pakistan (two years in each case), Tanganyika ($10

8 Gulick and Nelson, *op. cit.*, pp. 17–18.

9 President's Task Force on Foreign Economic Assistance, *The Act for International Development: A Program for the Decade of Development,* 1961, p. 13.

million over three years), Tunisia ($180 million over three years), and Nigeria ($250 million over the period of her Six-Year Plan). But A.I.D. has not on balance found this technique to be useful, and no new long-term commitments have been made since 1963. Because the Task Force stressed this technique so strongly and Congress was urged both in 1961 and later to strengthen the long-term commitment authority, the change in attitude calls for an explanation.

Administrative and operating problems account for part of the disenchantment with long-term commitments. The commitments usually covered all forms of A.I.D. assistance (and in some cases included Food for Peace), but did not specify the proportions of technical assistance, project loans, program loans, and (where applicable) food aid. Technical assistance accounted for a small part of the total, except in Nigeria. In any event recipient countries tend to discount or ignore technical assistance when considering the total volume of aid. As indicated earlier, well-prepared capital project proposals trickle in slowly, and the small number being considered for a specific country at any particular time may take a year or more to review. Because a long-term commitment is a promise to provide a specified total sum in a given time period, and because technical and capital assistance are not likely to absorb much of the commitment, the donor is placed under pressure to increase the volume of commodity assistance—perhaps beyond that which it feels is warranted in terms of balance-of-payments requirements. Alternatively, it can lower standards on projects to increase the flow of capital assistance. Neither choice is desirable. In a few cases friction over implementation of long-term commitments may have negated the good will and sense of mutual endeavor created by the initial announcement of the commitment.

More important, both the simple existence of the commitment and the probability of some misunderstanding regarding its implementation interfere with U.S. influence on self-help efforts. In other words, it has become clear that whatever value the prospect of a long-term commitment may have in inducing better *initial* planning for the next several years is outweighed by the commitment's effect in reducing *continuing* U.S. influence on current policy decisions during the period. The Task Force report discussed at length the variety of self-help measures needed under different circumstances, and emphasized the need for flexibility, but it returned again and again to the concept that the core of self-help was good long-term planning and programming. It followed logically that the multiyear commitment was an important tool. A.I.D. certainly would not belittle the importance of planning, but probably places greater emphasis than did the Task Force Report on month-to-month adjustment of policies and programs in response to changing circumstances and accumulated experience. Therefore, in those countries where the bulk of development assistance is concentrated, the major formal channel for U.S. influence is not the long-term commitment but the annual negotiations for program loans and in some cases more frequent joint reviews of the recipient country's progress and performance. Such reviews are valuable not only as a forum for exchange of views but also as an early warning system for spotting potential problems.

Of course, in many cases the United States is not the only nor even the major donor. Not only other bilateral donors but also the World Bank (IBRD), and its soft-loan affiliate, the International Development Association; the Inter-American Development Bank, the International Monetary Fund (IMF), and other multilateral institutions play an important role in many countries where the U.S. conducts sizeable assistance programs. Clearly, where more than one major donor is involved, coordination is important not only to avoid duplication or competition in providing resources, but also for constructive use of influence. At the very least, the recipient country should not have to cope with several different donors urging different and perhaps conflicting courses of action, nor should it be able to evade appropriate requirements by playing donors off against each other. Beyond this minimum degree of coordination, if all major donors can agree that certain self-help measures are feasible and desirable for a particular country, the prospect of persuading the country to act accordingly is enhanced.

In the past few years, interest in improved self-help has been a growing concern of all donors. The U.S. has taken the lead in the OECD's Development Assistance Committee (a forum for exchange of information and views among bilateral aid donors, primarily the Western European nations, Japan, and the United States) in working out a consensus on criteria for gauging self-help efforts and on the most useful techniques for identifying key self-help requirements.

The World Bank and the IMF are generally respected for their competence and are relatively free of suspicion of political motives,[10] although the IMF is not infrequently accused of ignoring the adverse

[10] There have been occasional allegations that one or both institutions are tools of the United States, reflecting both the fact that the United States is a majority shareholder in the IBRD and the IMF, and the frequent collaboration between the United States and the multilateral institutions to encourage improved policies in aid-receiving countries.

development effects of stabilization measures it recommends. Both organizations are effective channels of influence. The IMF usually takes the lead in advising member nations in financial difficulties regarding measures for stabilization, and in coordinating other lenders' policies toward such countries. IMF Stand-by Agreements usually require that the aided country attempt to obtain credit from other nations, and that their credit be extended on condition that the recipient observe the stipulations of the Stand-by. The United States has frequently worked closely with the Fund. The Greek stabilization program in the mid-1950's, and agreements with Brazil, Colombia, and Chile have all been supported by U.S. aid linked to observance of IMF recommendations. In Chile, for example, program loans in 1963 and 1964 were largely conditioned on Chilean compliance with fiscal, monetary, and foreign exchange rate policies defined in Stand-by Agreements with the IMF. More recently, in 1966–67, A.I.D. assistance to Ceylon and Ghana was tied to stabilization measures recommended by the Fund, and a similar pattern is probable in Indonesia.[11]

In the field of development measures, for years the World Bank has sent teams upon request to analyze prospects in a particular country, to assess its development plan, and to recommend appropriate policies. In the past few years the Bank has taken a more consistently active role not only in advising developing countries themselves but in coordinating donors' efforts. The IBRD sponsors donors' consortia for India and Pakistan, and chairs consultative groups for a number of other countries. The India and Pakistan Consortia, and a similar consortium for Turkey sponsored by the OECD, were originally established so that donors could agree on the countries' aid requirements. More recently, the consortia and consultative groups are being used to reach agreement not only on what is needed from donors but also on what would be appropriate to require of the recipient nation. For instance, the Bank played an important role in both urging and organizing support for India's import liberalization of 1965. Although complex controls were clearly stifling private sector growth, India found it difficult to dismantle the controls, both for ideological reasons—India had long been committed to a controlled and protective economy—and because it was not clear that foreign exchange would be available to cover the resulting increase in imports. After a long period of discussions, Indian Minister of Planning Asoka Mehta reached an understanding with World Bank President George Woods in April 1965. In response to India's decision, the Bank then took the lead in rounding

11 *New York Times,* January 5, 1967.

up increased assistance pledges, and succeeded in eliciting promises for a total of roughly $1.5 billion, including over $800 million in commodity assistance, for the first year of India's fourth Five-Year Plan. Previous years' pledges had reached about $1 billion in total aid of which $600 million was in commodity assistance.[12] The World Bank also took a leading role in encouraging India to take the still more major and difficult step of devaluing the rupee in June 1966.

Even where there is no formal consortium or consultative group, the United States has found it helpful to conduct negotiations for explicit self-help understandings parallel to, and where possible jointly with, negotiations between the recipient and the IMF (where stabilization is involved), the IBRD, other multilateral lending institutions, and other bilateral donors.

During the Marshall Plan period, the aided countries themselves brought pressure on each other for improved performance through the Organization for European Economic Cooperation (OEEC). Such an arrangement avoids the aura of tutelage—in the case of the developing countries, the fear of neocolonialism—and creates a sense of mutual endeavor. The closest analogy among the developing countries at the moment is the Inter-American Committee on the Alliance for Progress (CIAP), which was in part deliberately modeled on the Marshall Plan experience. CIAP conducts annual reviews of progress, policies, and plans of Latin American countries. Other regional organizations— perhaps the Economic Commission for Africa, the African Development Bank, and the Asian Development Bank—may assume similar functions as they build up their staffs and gain in experience and prestige.

The developing countries themselves increasingly accept the idea that donors have a legitimate interest in the development policies and programs of aid recipients. The representative of the World Bank at a recent unofficial conference on aid remarked that aided countries were now slower to complain of infringement of sovereignty than they had been in the past. He added that finance ministers in the developing countries sometimes incorporated agreements with the Bank on policy measures into their budget speeches.[13] There is a clear trend toward a more mature pattern of relationships based on the premise that development is a mutual endeavor, and that aid therefore is neither largesse

[12] *Washington Post,* June 22, 1965. These figures exclude very substantial Food for Peace assistance.

[13] Overseas Development Institute, *Effective Aid* (Report of an international conference held jointly by the Ditchley Foundation and ODI, June 3–6, 1966), p. 34.

for which gratitude or political favors is to be expected nor the just dues made available to the new nations from their former exploiters. But a great deal must still be learned on both sides.

Limits on the Effectiveness of External Influence

Although the use of aid as influence is still being explored, it is clear that major constraints limit its potential effectiveness. A donor may be reluctant to jeopardize political or security foreign policy objectives in a particular country by pressing too hard for improved development policies. For example, the United States almost certainly has been more restrained in encouraging improved development policies in Turkey because of a desire to maintain continued Turkish military cooperation.

Inadequate understanding of the development process itself, and of the specific factors at work in a particular country, also limits effective external influence on self-help efforts. In several outstanding cases, the combined analysis and judgment of the governments themselves and of multilateral and bilateral donors, coupled with vigorous implementation of agreed measures, failed to bring about the expected results. As in some branches of medicine, a good deal is understood about causes and there are some fairly effective means of controlling symptoms, but no real cures to persistent problems have been discovered. For example, in Chile at the end of 1962, a decade of inflation had caused severe dislocations and prevented growth. Early in 1963, Chile's largest foreign lenders, the World Bank, the IMF, and the United States, agreed to continue to provide assistance only after the Government of Chile committed itself to major policy changes to assure some degree of financial stability. During the next three years, assistance was provided contingent on specific major reforms agreed upon by Chile and the major donors. Chile enacted major tax reforms in February 1964, overhauled its internal revenue service, and reassessed all urban and rural real estate taxes. Central bank credit expansion was held within agreed limits, a flexible exchange rate policy was used, and autonomous agencies sharply increased their savings. The Government accumulated large surpluses on current account, reducing the total level of spending while maintaining development investments. Yet the cost of living continued to rise. Explicit leverage linked to precise targets was effective in the narrow sense, but failed to achieve its real goal.[14] Simi-

---

[14] Gulick and Nelson, *op. cit.,* p. 22ff.

larly, stabilization measures in Brazil succeeded in temporarily halting inflation, but at the price of recession.

The shakiness of our prescriptions is surely cause for caution. Many observers and practitioners would go further, and argue that because donors do not necessarily know best, and may disagree among themselves, it is doubtful whether they should "back their judgments with their power and money." [15] However, the question is not really whether donors' judgment can solve all problems, but whether their analysis and recommendations taken jointly with host country judgment can encourage better policies than would otherwise be adopted. On balance, this has almost certainly been the case.

A third basic constraint on the potential effectiveness of external influence is recipient governments' limited political and administrative capacity. The less secure and stable a government, the weaker its ability to formulate and carry out needed measures. Thus, as noted earlier, external influence tends to be least effective where improved policies and programs are most urgent. In such circumstances the United States may focus its efforts on narrower reforms which require less administrative sophistication.

Even where administrative competence is not a major problem, internal political pressures obviously remain an important constraint on economic reform. The issue of rice subsidies in Ceylon is a case in point. Elections in April 1965 in that country gave a narrow victory to Dudley Senanayake over the incumbent Communist-supported government of Sirimavo Bandaranaike. The new Prime Minister inherited a set of difficult economic problems, including a budget deficit running near $120 million, of which roughly $100 million could be attributed to high rice subsidies. Under the subsidy system, the government buys rice from the farmer at twice the world market price and sells it, in turn, to the consumer at a third or a quarter of the procurement price. Moreover, the budgetary impact of the subsidy grows annually, reflecting population growth: the cost increased by $3.5 million in 1966 over the $106 million bill incurred in 1965, and by $9 million over the original projection in the 1965 budget.[16] The World Bank has strongly urged a phased five-year reduction in the subsidies. But Mr. Senanayake thus far has resisted this particular reform, mindful of his experience as premier a decade earlier, when he cut subsidies and was promptly voted out of office. He has, however, been responsive to Bank advice on other points. Specifically to balance the rice subsidy,

[15] Overseas Development Institute, *op. cit.*, p. 33.
[16] Selig Harrison, *Washington Post*, May 26, 1966.

the Ceylonese Government has raised the price of government-distributed wheat flour. The budget also imposes substantial new taxes and provides for increased noninflationary local borrowing, thus while financing new growth programs, keeping the budget deficit well below the $100 million ceiling regarded as permissible in the 1965 World Bank White Paper.[17]

In a second recent instance, donors may have verged on excessive pressure for politically sensitive reforms. Inadequate foreign exchange has hampered progress in Colombia for a number of years, due partly to low world prices for the coffee on which Colombia relies for roughly three fourths of her export earnings. To conserve foreign exchange, Colombia imposed complex import licensing controls and a multiple exchange rate system. Economists in A.I.D. and the World Bank criticized the controls and aspects of the multiple exchange rate system on grounds that they distorted the pattern of trade and internal development. Devaluation, in principle preferable in terms of long-term effects, often has painful short-run consequences. Colombia had devalued in 1962 and again in 1965; the first effort was largely vitiated by price and wage increases, and the second led by spring of 1966 to strong pressure on Colombia's foreign exchange reserves. In August 1966, Carlos Lleras Restrepo took office as Colombia's President. Lleras had some economic training and was expected to provide much firmer and more vigorous policy leadership than his predecessor. He did indeed move rapidly to improve planning, policies and programs. However, major donors urged measures to extend substantially the devaluation begun the previous September, although Lleras had made it plain he felt such measures were politically too sensitive to risk. In autumn 1966, the World Bank and the IMF rather suddenly hardened their position and insisted that their support was contingent on devaluation. Lleras announced in a major speech in November 1966 that Colombia would forego their assistance and instead would conserve exchange by reimposing import licensing and introducing extensive exchange controls. Although the new measures included important desirable aspects such as a required registration of Colombian assets abroad (intended to control capital flight), on balance the approach was likely to impede and distort long-term development. However, four months later, Lleras installed a new foreign exchange system that amounted to a partial devaluation. The IMF promptly authorized a $60 million stand-by loan, and in late May A.I.D. extended a $100

---

[17] *Washington Post,* August 22, 1966.

million loan.[18] It is hard to say whether political opposition cooled, or Lleras' initial resistance was primarily a feint designed to win domestic political support. Probably both factors were at work.[19]

Excessive external pressure runs two alternative dangers. Such pressure may strain a government beyond its capacity and thereby weaken it. Alternatively, the government may reject the advice, confronting donors with the choice of withholding aid or undermining their own credibility. As an excellent *Washington Post* editorial observed with reference to Ceylon, "Reform recommended solely on the basis of economic criteria and pursued before a country has been psychologically prepared could undermine the political foundations on which development rests. And the repeated rejection of politically untenable reform recommendations could in time tarnish the Bank's well-earned prestige." [20] The point clearly applies equally to other donors. Unfortunately, the superstructure of some of the more successful instances of influence—conditions, agreements, quarterly reviews—is more readily visible than the patiently laid foundation of discussion and consensus between recipient and donors. Therefore, successful instances of aid-induced reform carry the danger of encouraging donors to rely increasingly on mechanistic devices.

A fourth constraint on the effectiveness of external influence may turn out to be the reluctance of donors to provide the level of support required by major reforms in the larger developing countries. Economists estimate that a substantial increase—perhaps a doubling—of total aid over the next few years is essential if a number of countries to which we have serious commitments are to continue to increase per capita incomes.[21] Analysts both within and outside the U.S. Government have argued that if India were to dismantle its complex controls not only of imports but also of foreign exchange, agriculture, and other fields, and to take the additional measures needed for an eventual breakthrough to self-sustaining growth, this would create a temporary

[18] *New York Times,* April 15 and May 29, 1967.

[19] Lleras' position rallied strong political support. In December, shortly after his speech, the Colombian Congress passed a major increase in gasoline taxes. Potentially much more important, the Congress voted (by the required two-thirds majority) to reduce the majority required for certain types of legislation including administrative reorganization and fiscal reform from two-thirds of the Congress to a simple majority, thereby temporarily removing a paralyzing constitutional requirement.

[20] *Washington Post,* August 22, 1966.

[21] Edward S. Mason, *Foreign Aid and Foreign Policy,* Harper & Row, New York, 1964, p. 6.

need for a doubled volume of external aid.[22] U.S. assistance to India during the five-year period 1962 to 1966 averaged a bit under $1 billion a year—roughly half A.I.D.-financed and half in Food for Peace commodities. Recently India has indeed devalued the rupee and taken measures to liberalize the economy, and the Consortium is being called upon to respond accordingly. India is the largest prospective claimant, but other countries may also be able to absorb large amounts of aid productively if they take needed reform measures. For instance, if Indonesia's new regime succeeds in stabilizing the economy, renegotiating debts, and adopting sound development programs, Indonesia will need and warrant substantial aid.

The question is one of the advanced nations' will to support effective development efforts, not their capacity to do so. No advanced nation devotes more than 1 per cent of its national income to foreign assistance, and the United States has recently spent less than one third of 1 per cent of its income on aid. Nor is adverse impact on donors' balance of payments a serious consideration, because the United States and most other donors require that aid be spent, with rare exceptions, on goods and services they produce.

If donors are to place increased emphasis on self-help efforts in aid-receiving countries, they must be prepared to respond to improved efforts with the volume and forms of assistance appropriate to the reform itself and to the development opportunities and requirements created by reform. Such a policy might well prove not only morally appropriate but less expensive over the long run. Economic analysis suggests that for many countries a more rapid development path may demand higher annual levels of assistance for a few years than does slower growth, but that the cumulative aid bill to the point where the country has reached self-sustaining growth may be less for the fast-moving country than for one that makes more gradual progress stretched over a longer period of time. In other words, providing more aid for a short time may reduce total aid required for take-off. However, thus far the U.S. Government and public (as well as other donor nations) seem much readier to press for more self-help from the developing nations than to accept the implied obligations—and opportunities—of exercising their influence.

External donors thus assume a heavy burden of responsibility when they intervene vigorously and on a continuing basis in a developing country's policy formation. This is not to argue against such interven-

[22] *Washington Post,* June 24, 1965.

tion. As we have seen, external influence may be extremely useful as a counterweight to internal resistance to needed change, as a supplement to analytic capacity in countries lacking their own trained analysts, and as a stimulant to fresh perspectives in more sophisticated countries. But effective use of influence also demands recognition of the limits of our understanding of development problems, the patience to work toward a consensus on goals and means, and the willingness to stand by the implicit obligations of the game. It is not yet clear that the United States—or other donors—can consistently meet these standards.

CHAPTER 5

Using Aid for Short-Run Political Purposes

THE USE OF AID for short-run political purposes is probably the most controversial aspect of the foreign aid effort. President Kennedy's Task Force on Foreign Economic Assistance stated in its 1961 guidelines for a revamped program:

> The whole program must be conceived of as an effort, stretching over a considerable number of years, to alter the basic social and economic conditions in the less developed world. It must be recognized as a slow-acting tool designed to prevent political and military crises such as those recently confronted in Laos and Cuba. It is not a tool for dealing with these crises after they have erupted.[1]

The Task Force recommended including among the instruments of aid a Supporting Assistance category designated for short-run security and political objectives. Among such goals it specifically listed defense support, access to bases, economic stability under crisis circumstances, and an alternative to excessive reliance on Communist sources of aid.[2] However, the Task Force proposed a substantial shift in emphasis away from such objectives toward economic and social development.

Congress endorsed this guidance in the 1961 Foreign Assistance Act. Two years later it reasserted the primacy of development objectives, stating:

> It is the sense of the Congress that in the administration of assistance [financed from Development Loan or Technical Assistance funds], every possible precaution should be taken to assure that such assistance is not diverted to short-term emergency purposes (such as budgetary purposes, balance of payments purposes, or military purposes) or any other purpose not essential to the long-range economic development of recipient countries.[3]

Congress has also consistently pressed for reduction of the amount of Supporting Assistance within the total aid program and for confining its use to a short list of countries.

---

[1] President's Task Force on Foreign Economic Assistance, *The Act for International Development: A Program for the Decade of Development*, 1961, p. 12.

[2] *Ibid.*, p. 55.

[3] Foreign Assistance Act of 1963, Section 101(c)(3), amending Section 102 of the 1961 Act.

A.I.D. has indeed emphasized development. But substantial sums continue to go for security purposes, and many aid actions—though only a small fraction of total A.I.D. funds—are designed to serve immediate political objectives. A great deal of criticism has been directed to the use of aid for short-run political purposes; some, but not all, of the critics also deplore the use of economic aid for security purposes. For example, Senator Wayne Morse (Democrat, Oregon) dissenting from the majority report of the Senate Foreign Relations Committee on the 1964 Foreign Assistance Act, argued:

My difference with much of the program is over what really does serve the interests of the United States. I do not believe that aid extended for military reasons, security reasons, or for reasons of political intrigue serves our long-run interests—and this is a long-run program.[4]

A report on aid prepared by the Critical Issues Council of the Republican Citizens' Committee, chaired by Dr. Milton S. Eisenhower, states:

The heart of the problem [is] . . . the failure, waste, and ineffectiveness arising out of the use of aid for shortrun political purposes . . . a multipurpose gadget to be taken out of the kit as found convenient—a kind of bribe or bludgeon to accomplish any and all kinds of foreign policy purposes.[5]

Professor Hans Morgenthau argues that although using aid for political purposes is neither immoral nor impractical, our efforts to date have been clumsy and ineffective.

. . . Aid has been conceived as a self-sufficient technical enterprise covering a multitude of disparate objectives and activities, responding haphazardly to all sorts of demands, sound and unsound, unrelated or only by accident related to the political purposes of our foreign policy.[6]

Before assessing the validity of these criticisms and the assumptions on which they are based, it will be useful to have more clearly in mind the range of political uses to which U.S. economic aid is put and some impression of its effectiveness in a sample of past instances.[7]

---

[4] Foreign Assistance Act of 1964: Individual Views of Senator Morse on H.R. 11380, 88th Congress, 2d Session, Senate Report 1188, Part 2, p. 1.

[5] Critical Issues Council, Republican Citizens' Committee, "The Future of Foreign Aid," inserted in the *Congressional Record,* June 4, 1964, pp. 12302–6.

[6] Hans Morgenthau, "A Political Theory of Foreign Aid," *American Political Science Review,* Vol. LVI, No. 2, June 1962, p. 301.

[7] The cases discussed here have been selected partly because they illustrate clear-cut types of goals, but the sample also includes some cases in which the purpose of the aid action might be interpreted in more than one way. There are also many cases in which the U.S. action reflects one major motive plus several subsidiary ones.

Influencing Internal Politics

Between 1961 and 1966, aid (or the withholding of aid) was used to:

1. Buy time for new regimes to consolidate their position and formulate programs of action.
2. Bolster governments faced with acute financial crises, due either to special and temporary problems or to chronic conditions.
3. Relieve politically threatening unemployment, or counter other specific political threats.
4. Attempt to influence the outcome of elections, or to ensure that the elections are held.
5. Register disapproval of military coups and encourage the early scheduling of elections.
6. On rare occasions, to attempt to alter the composition of a government, outside the context of elections.

All these purposes relate to the recipient's short-run internal political situation.

Emergency Support in Economic Crises

Single-shot budget and/or balance-of-payments support is the most frequently used means of giving a new government a chance to get organized, and of bolstering regimes faced with financial crises. In either circumstance, the government finds that it is acutely short of foreign exchange or local revenues or both. It owes money to local suppliers of goods and services, and may be weeks or months behind in paying civil servants, teachers, and the armed forces. If the situation continues, imported capital and consumer goods become scarce and prices rise. There may be strikes and demonstrations, and muttering from the armed forces about the need to save the country from disaster.

Examples are legion of new regimes facing staggering inherited problems of budgetary deficits, inflation or depression, and foreign exchange shortages. Some of the clear-cut instances in which the United States has extended aid to provide a breathing space include:

—A $25 million Supporting Assistance loan to the Dominican Republic in January 1962. The remnants of the Trujillo regime had been decisively overthrown in December, but the new interim Council of State was faced with a looted Treasury.[8]

—$50 million from the Contingency Fund for Brazil in June 1964.[9] The Goulart regime had been overthrown in March, leaving the new Branco government (among other problems) an incredible anticipated budget deficit and an inflation running at an annual rate of 140 per cent in the first quarter of 1964. The new Government was formulating a program for stabilization and development, but if aid were delayed until the program was complete, the problems would have been compounded.

—In spring 1965, $5.8 million from the Contingency Fund to bolster the government of Prime Minister Forbes Burnham of Guyana, who had defeated Marxist Cheddi Jagan at the polls the previous December. Burnham's government was drawing up a long-range development plan designed to relieve explosive racial tensions between Indians and Negroes, but needed assistance in financing job-creating public works as an immediate means to this end.[10]

A government that has been in office for some time may face a temporary budget or balance-of-payments crisis resulting either from factors beyond its control, such as the failure of a key export crop or a change in world market prices, or from economically unwise measures taken in response to temporary political pressures. In 1962 the Government of Colombia relaxed import controls before a national election; a balance of payments crisis resulted. In this case the United States extended $30 million in Supporting Assistance.[11] In another set of circumstances, a government may be making an honest attempt to cope with grave problems, but necessary economic reforms may have an initial effect of undercutting political support. In Honduras in mid-1963, the Villeda Government, despite courageous measures, faced a serious budget deficit aggravated by the impact of Central American economic integration agreements. The regime was under heavy rightist political attack. In June (after having held back for some months pending Honduran reforms), the United States agreed to provide $2 million in Supporting Assistance.[12] In Iran in autumn 1961 the United States feared that a financial crisis might bring down the

[8] *New York Times,* January 11 and 23, 1962.
[9] *Ibid.,* June 25, 1964.
[10] *Ibid.,* March 5, 1965.
[11] A.I.D. press release dated April 12, 1962.
[12] *Washington Post,* October 11, 1963.

reform-minded government of Prime Minister Ali Amini, which had taken office in May;[13] $14 million in Supporting Assistance from the Contingency Fund was made available.[14]

Much more controversial in principle are situations where an established government, due to inexperience, incompetence, or indifference, seems unable to narrow a chronic deficit, or even aggravates the problem by irresponsible policies and spending. Although support of such a regime is clearly undesirable, the United States may believe that the alternative to the current government is either chaos or a worse regime. Thus the United States provided $8 million in budget support from the Contingency Fund to Ecuador in November 1961, and $7 million in 1962. In the first instance, there were extenuating circumstances. Although the Velasco administration was known to be corrupt and inept, falling prices for coffee, bananas and cocoa had contributed to a foreign exchange pinch. In the second instance, declining exchange reserves and government revenues threatened the weak administration of Carlos Julio Arosemena Monroy. Although the United States had little enthusiasm for the regime, it saw no better prospects should Arosemena fall.[15]

All these aid actions were intended to counter an immediate threat and to restore a modicum of political and economic stability. Wherein do they differ from the security-stability programs described in Chapter 2? The first distinction lies in the nature of the threat. In Vietnam, Laos, and Northeast Thailand, and in the Congo in the early 1960's, insurgents seek to overthrow the government by force. In Jordan, bitter revanchist Palestinian refugees, spurred by external Arab support, constitute a continuing threat to stability; in Bolivia general political turbulence and the specific problem of armed and extremist-led tin miners in control of the key industry of the nation create a chronic danger. Reflecting the more structured and continuing nature of the threat in these countries, A.I.D.'s programs provide continuing budget and balance-of-payments support. There is no expectation that these security/stability programs are single-shot actions; rather, they reflect a judgment that a sustained input is necessary because the political collapse of the countries concerned would substantially damage U.S. interests.

The short-run "bail-out" actions are, in contrast, intended as one-time measures to achieve specific goals. Therefore, it is fair to judge

[13] *New York Times,* May 31, June 6, August 4, 1961.
[14] A.I.D. press release dated February 16, 1962.
[15] *Washington Evening Star,* May 2, 1965.

their effectiveness in short-run terms rather than over a period of years. The 1962 loan to the Dominican Republic interim regime served its immediate purpose of bolstering the economy at a politically delicate moment, permitting the Council of State to consolidate control and prepare for elections while containing far-left elements. Without a prompt loan on lenient terms, the Council might have fallen either to Castro-oriented groups or to another rightist military coup, which in turn might well have led ultimately to an extreme-left takeover. Later events leading up to and including the overthrow of the elected government in 1963 do not qualify the success of the loan in terms of its immediate purpose.

Similarly, after the emergency loan of June 1964, the Brazilian Government successfully negotiated debt rescheduling agreements with European creditor governments, Japan, and the United States; entered into an IMF Stand-by Agreement; and drew up and presented to the Inter-American Committee for the Alliance for Progress a stabilization and development program covering the period through 1966.[16] Since then, it has become clear that the measures controlled inflation at the price of recession, and that efforts to gain development momentum have had only marginal success. Nonetheless, the June 1964 loan succeeded in buying time for the government to organize its program.

In Guyana, in 1965, Burnham's new Negro-dominated government instituted a sizeable road-building program, locating some of the roads in the largely Indian area of the Courentyne. As an interim measure, Burnham also instructed the Rice Marketing Board to continue paying rice farmers (most of whom are Indian) the subsidized rice price introduced by his Indian predecessor, former Premier Jagan. Relative to a total budget of about $45 million, the $5 million U.S. grant represented substantial support for such programs. However, other measures, which required no financial input (albeit considerable political courage), may have had as great an effect in easing racial tension. For instance, the heretofore largely Negro police force was instructed to draw 75 per cent of its recruits for the next five years from the Indian population and to change its physical requirements, which had previously eliminated many Indian applicants.[17]

The June 1963 decision to extend budget assistance to Honduras achieved certain immediate economic goals, averting a threatened run

[16] Clarence Gulick and Joan Nelson, "Promoting Effective Development Policies: A.I.D. Experience in the Developing Countries," A.I.D. Discussion Paper No. 9, September 1965, pp. 18–19.

[17] Donald L. Horowitz, "Pigment Politics in the Newest Nation," manuscript version of article published in the *New Leader,* July 4, 1966.

on government bonds and renewing business confidence. However, the government was slow to meet conditions precedent to disbursing the loan. Villeda was toppled by a coup in October 1963, just ten days before scheduled elections in which his Liberal Party appeared likely to win a fresh mandate. The $2 million in Supporting Assistance had not yet been disbursed, and was withheld along with other pending assistance after the coup.[18] The simple announcement of budget support may have helped gain support for the Villeda regime, but by that same token may have hastened the decision of the army and the opposition National Party that a coup was preferable to defeat at the polls. In the case of Iran, Ali Amini resigned as Premier in July 1962, blaming insufficient U.S. aid for his failure to close the budget gap.[19] However, many of the reforms launched during his tenure were continued.

While the cases of Honduras and Iran are ambiguous, the least successful pair of cases in this sample of crisis budgetary assistance are those where the rationale was weakest initially: the loans to Ecuador. The Arosemena regime made virtually no progress in meeting the country's problems, and was overthrown by a military coup in June 1963. The military regime proved much more competent in adopting and carrying out needed measures, including tax reform and financial consolidation, and also promised to hold elections as soon as necessary reforms were under way. It is interesting to speculate whether events would have taken this course sooner had the United States not bolstered the Arosemena Government.

Unemployment and Union Politics

Aid has also been used to address more specific political problems, such as high unemployment in a particular area or group or potential Communist domination of particular labor unions. For example, while visiting the United States in autumn 1961, President Prado of Peru asked President Kennedy for emergency assistance to provide employment relief for some 30,000 persons in the Puno area. The area had suffered severe drought; the Peruvian Government feared that resulting poverty and unemployment would lead to political extremism and possible violence. President Kennedy agreed to provide the assistance, and a $6 million Supporting Assistance loan was made available, to cover roughly half the costs of wages, small tools, and supplies for work projects.[20] However, release of the aid was contingent on satis-

---

18 *Washington Post,* October 11, 1963.
19 *New York Times,* July 19, 1962.
20 A.I.D. press release dated February 9, 1962.

factory projects being worked out. The rate of utilization turned out to be slow, only a fraction of the sum was actually expended, and the remaining funds were deobligated after a year.

As mentioned earlier, a more endemic unemployment problem in Kenya is being attacked through a National Youth Service. The United States has provided roughly $2.7 million in assistance to the Service in the past two years, including construction equipment and tools, uniforms, tents and other supplies, and vocational education instructors. As of autumn 1966 the corps numbered 5,000; there are plans to expand enrollment to 7,000 men and an equal number of young women.[21] It is too soon to assess the results of the Service; however, demonstrations in Nairobi by unemployed youths have tapered off since 1965.

Sitraterco, the Honduran union of employees of the Tela Railroad (a subsidiary of the United Fruit Company), had strongly fought Communist infiltration. In March 1963, A.I.D. provided $400,000 in Supporting Assistance directly to Sitraterco to finance union housing, thereby bolstering the union. Even though United Fruit provides free housing for many of its workers, the importance of the union housing is suggested by one worker's comment: "This is the first thing I will ever have owned." [22]

Elections

Although direct and obvious use of aid to support preferred candidates in national elections would be likely to backfire, aid has been used in various indirect ways to try to influence electoral results, or simply to ensure that the elections are held. U.S. support for the Venezuelan military and police was stepped up to help control terrorist efforts to sabotage the elections of 1963. This action undoubtedly made a modest contribution to the outcome. Despite repeated terrorist incidents before the election and specific threats to snipe at voters, 95 per cent of the voters participated,[23] six party nominees and an independent competed for votes, and Venezuela accomplished its first transfer of power from one constitutionally elected President to another.[24]

In some instances the United States has been concerned that a pre-election economic crisis would cause discontent, which might hurt moderate candidates. In Chile in spring of 1964, Socialist and Commu-

21   *Washington Post,* August 18, 1966.
22   *Ibid.,* October 12, 1963.
23   *Christian Science Monitor,* December 5, 1963.
24   *New York Times,* March 10, 1964.

nist-supported Salvador Allende was given a strong chance of winning the national elections scheduled for September—perhaps the sole case where a Marxist candidate appeared likely to win in free elections in a major Latin American country. Allende was opposed by a reformist and dynamic Christian Democratic candidate, Eduardo Frei. The United States feared that renewed inflationary pressure in Chile would increase support for Allende,[25] and in May loaned Chile $15 million for commodity imports. Although the loan was part of a continuing program of support for Chile in response to serious stabilization efforts, desire to dampen the inflation in the pre-election period by financing additional imports almost certainly played a role in the timing and volume of the U.S. decision. What effect this may have had on the outcome of the election is impossible to ascertain, but Frei won by a lopsided margin.

In Bolivia, the U.S. Embassy openly supported President Paz Estenssoro in his bid for re-election in March 1964, believing he was the only political figure capable of preventing anarchy. Although no U.S. decisions to support new projects or provide additional aid seem to have been taken to influence the election, Ambassador Henderson used inauguration of Alliance projects to demonstrate support for Paz, frequently scheduling such appearances to coincide with rallies during the campaign. Paz won the election (all opposition candidates withdrew, calling on voters to abstain from voting) but was overthrown by the military in November of that year.[26]

Coups

Delaying recognition and withholding assistance has become virtually a ritual U.S. response to military coups in Latin America. Chronologically, since 1962 the United States has used this means of registering disapproval and encouraging the early scheduling of elections in Argentina (March 1962), Peru (July 1962), Guatemala (March 1963), the Dominican Republic (September 1963), Honduras (October 1963), Bolivia (November 1964), and again in Argentina (June 1966). The technique was also used to discourage an abortive coup in the Dominican Republic in January 1962. U.S. assistance was not yet under way (the remnants of the Trujillo regime had left the country only the previous November), but an economic assistance agreement had been signed with the newly installed Council of State and a U.S. assistance team was in the Dominican Republic surveying

---

[25] *Ibid.*, March 31, April 12, 1964.
[26] *Ibid.*, August 9, November 22, 1964.

possible projects when the attempted coup occurred.[27] The team was promptly withdrawn and it was made clear that the United States did not recognize the military-civil junta;[28] a counter-coup reinstalled the Council of State within a matter of days.[29]

The U.S. responses to the coups of July 1963 in Ecuador and March 1964 in Brazil were exceptions to this pattern of withholding recognition. In the case of Ecuador, military officers of middle-class background moved against President Arosemena, whose inept administration had brought development efforts virtually to a halt; the legislature was paralyzed by political infighting, and Communist activities had been stepped up. The junta promptly announced that it would pass laws on agrarian reform, the civil service, the penal code, and other long-neglected fields, and promised to hold elections with two years, although no specific date was set. In Brazil, the United States made no effort to conceal its delight at the replacement of the Goulart regime, under which Brazil's economic and political situation had deteriorated rapidly. In neither case was U.S. aid interrupted, and in Brazil the United States shortly provided substantial commodity assistance.

The more standard U.S. pattern, however, has been to withhold recognition and aid until the new junta announced a plan for elections. Elections were in fact held in Argentina 16 months after the 1962 coup (Peronist candidates were barred); in Peru after a year; in Guatemala only after three years; in Bolivia after about 18 months; in Ecuador after three years; and in Brazil for members of Congress after 32 months. In Honduras a Constitutional Assembly was elected in 1965, and later in the year promulgated a Constitution, declared itself a National Assembly, and elected the chief of the military junta to a six-year term as President.

Halting aid and withdrawing the A.I.D. mission may disrupt aid programs for considerably longer than the actual period of suspension. In the Dominican Republic, for example, the United States withheld recognition and aid from October to December 1963, but the administrative and technical problems created by the withdrawal meant that aid programs did not really resume operations until the following April. The six-month pause caused considerable hardship in the Republic, and at least one highly placed official, former

---

[27] *Ibid.*, January 8, 17, 1962.

[28] *Ibid.*, January 18, 1962.

[29] *Ibid.*, January 19, 20, 1962. See also Abraham Lowenthal, "Foreign Aid as a Political Instrument: The Case of the Dominican Republic," in *Public Policy*, Vol. XIV, 1965, pp. 145–146.

Assistant Secretary of State for Inter-American Affairs Jack Vaughn, has stated that in retrospect, he believes the suspension may have been a mistake.[30]

The U.S. policy has not succeeded in counteracting Latin American suspicions that the U.S. military and the CIA are often covert supporters of military coups. Despite repeated official White House and State Department statements and actual U.S. behavior, former President Frondizi of Argentina,[31] and spokesmen for Paz Estenssoro of Bolivia, Bosch of the Dominican Republic [32] and Villeda of Honduras [33] have accused the United States of complicity or at least tacit acquiescence in their overthrow. However, in general the U.S. approach has won approval from Latin American governments. The policy has obviously not succeeded in preventing coups, but it has probably played a modest role in supplementing more basic factors that discourage them, such as the shift in the social origin of the officer corps in many Latin American countries and a more general broadening of the bases of political power. Moreover, the U.S. approach may have had considerably more effect in moderating juntas' policies and speeding the return to civilian government than in deterring coups in the first place.

Changing the Composition of the Government

On very rare occasions U.S. economic assistance has been used to encourage or virtually force a change in government composition, outside the context of elections. Withholding of aid played a role in the events leading up to the coup of November 1, 1963, in Vietnam. From the beginning of that year, Buddhist and student protest against the policies of Ngo Dinh Nhu had grown increasingly bitter and widespread. The regime's repressive tactics not only failed to restore order but also aroused strong criticism in the United States and other nations. From early September, the possibility of cutting U.S. economic aid to force the ouster of Ngo and a change in policies was openly debated. President Kennedy discussed the question on television on September 8, at that time stating that he felt such a move would be ill-advised.[34] However, the situation continued to deteriorate and in early October the United States suspended the commercial (commodity) import program.[35] Although the U.S. action

---

[30] *Washington Post,* February 10, 1966.
[31] *New York Times,* May 26, November 22, 1964.
[32] *Ibid.,* November 22, 1964.
[33] *Washington Post,* January 24, 1965.
[34] *New York Times,* September 10, 1963.
[35] *Ibid.,* October 8, 1963.

unquestionably would have had far-reaching economic consequences had it been long continued, in fact the aid suspension probably acted primarily as a clear indication to groups within Vietnam of U.S. Government views on the crisis. The Ngo regime was over-thrown on November 1. The U.S. Government recognized the new government a week later, and promptly opened discussions on resumption of the commodity import program.[36]

Other cases of this kind are less clear-cut, and certainly were not the subject of open public and Congressional debate. It seems fairly clear that U.S. commodity aid to Laos, which finances a very large part of the country's total imports, was suspended for some months in 1962 "as part of efforts to force the conservative govern-ment of Prince Boun Oum to accept the formation of a coalition government with neutralist and Communist political leaders and thus to end the losing battle against leftist guerrillas." [37]

The examples given make clear the heavy concentration in the Latin American region of efforts to influence internal political affairs. The United States has not generally reacted to military coups in Africa and Asia by withholding recognition and withdrawing aid.[38] Although several countries outside the Western hemisphere receive continuing U.S. budget support, single-shot bail-out efforts are rarer than in Latin America. The pattern obviously reflects stronger U.S. interests in Latin America. It may also reflect the view that democratic institutions are more developed and have deeper roots in Latin America, with its heritage of European cultural and political values, than in most other parts of the developing world. Therefore it is worthwhile not only to promote democratic evolution indirectly through long-term assistance for economic growth but also to preserve democratic institutions in more immediate and direct ways. More frequent U.S. action is also a result of the fact that the United States provides the great preponderance of all aid reaching Latin America; in Africa, British or French reactions would be far more influential than U.S. measures.

This survey of ways in which U.S. economic assistance has been used to influence internal political events in the recipient country

---

[36] *Ibid.*, November 8, 1963.

[37] *Wall Street Journal,* August 29, 1963.

[38] The United States responded to the military coup of April 1967 in Greece by withholding major items of military equipment scheduled under the military assistance program. A.I.D. assistance to Greece had been terminated in 1964. *New York Times,* May 17, 1967.

excludes many actions designed to affect the course of long-run political evolution by altering the attitudes of key groups, strengthening voluntary and local organizations, and the like. These are discussed in Chapter 6. Both the purpose and the techniques of assistance for political development have more in common with aid for economic development than with the short-run, single-shot, limited-purpose actions discussed here. However, the line between aid to influence the short-run political situation and aid to affect long-run political trends is not always easy to draw. Often the basic reason for attempting to influence the course of immediate political events is to preserve the opportunity for constructive political and economic evolution in the long run.

Influencing Recipients' Foreign Policies

As the brief survey in Chapter 1 suggested, aid has been used over the past five years to try to influence three aspects of recipient countries' foreign policies: their bilateral relations with the United States; their Cold War attitudes and roles; and their behavior toward their neighbors and in international organizations outside of the Cold War context.

Good Will Toward the United States

Among aid techniques designed primarily to further good bilateral relations with the United States, Independence Day gifts are the most obvious and noncontroversial. The history of diplomacy includes a long tradition of governments presenting other governments with gifts on appropriate occasions; foreign assistance merely provides a convenient way of financing an established practice. As various African nations have become independent, the United States has usually marked the occasion by announcing a gift—bookmobiles or mobile health units (for Mali, Senegal, Sierra Leone, among others); scholarships (Congo, Rwanda, Burundi, Guinea); a library of technical films (Cameroons); and in a few instances, a light airplane to permit government officials to reach isolated parts of the country (Dahomey, Somali Republic, Upper Volta, Botswana). If unusually large gifts to Ghana (a technical library) and the Congo (300 scholarships) are excluded, the average cost per country has been about $70,000. Many of the gifts were given in connection with broader A.I.D.-financed developmental projects or activities. However, marking the occasion of independence with an aid-funded gift does not necessarily mean the United States will provide continuing assistance. Recent gifts to newly independent Lesutho (formerly Basutoland) and Botswana (formerly Bechuanaland) carry no such implication.

The Mission Director's or Self-Help Fund is a second technique designed essentially to win good will. The director of each A.I.D. mission abroad has the authority to use up to a specified amount [39] each year to finance small projects that seem worthy of support. Periodic reports must be submitted on the uses made of the fund. Usually it is used to buy materials or equipment to support private self-help efforts, for instance, rental of a truck to carry gravel for surfacing an access road built by villagers; equipment for a clinic started at the initiative of a voluntary organization. Such projects clearly contribute to economic and social progress, both directly and by encouraging broader participation and more local initiative in development processes. The decision to give the directors this authority was probably based both on the desire to be able to respond quickly and flexibly to worthwhile small-scale host country initiatives, and on the belief that such assistance may generate more good will toward the United States than do much larger development projects.

The desire to provide aid in forms that appeal directly to large numbers of people also occasionally leads to larger-scale "impact projects." An impact project is designed to demonstrate the donor's good will and interest in the country. The classic illustrations are some of the projects financed by the Soviet Union and Communist China: sports stadia in Burma and Guinea, or the paving of the streets of Kabul in Afghanistan. But impact projects need not be devoid of developmental merit. The Cambodian-American Friendship Highway was clearly an impact project, but was also expected to contribute to economic growth. Projects designed to contribute immediately to the welfare of the population at large or of specific groups, without contributing much to growth, can also be viewed as impact projects. The desire to have an impact on groups judged to be politically restless and potentially powerful is certainly an element in U.S. support for low-cost urban housing programs in Colombia and elsewhere. The boundary between the welfare type of impact project and humanitarian aid is blurred: there are obvious impact overtones to Russian financing of hospitals in Kenya and

---

[39] During fiscal year 1967, up to $50,000 for each post. Starting in fiscal year 1968, the U.S. Ambassadors in certain African posts where other bilateral U.S. assistance has been phased out will be authorized to use up to $200,000 for projects meeting Self-Help Fund criteria.

Guinea, or U.S. financing of the measles inoculations campaign in West Africa.

"Pet projects" are still another way in which aid is occasionally used to promote good relations and diplomatic access. A Prime Minister or some other key political leader may set his heart upon a particular project and press hard for U.S. support. Clear-cut pet projects, that is, projects where the primary justification plainly is one of pleasing a key official, are extremely rare. Less clear-cut cases are undoubtedly more frequent, such as a proposed project that is less than top priority but has some merit in developmental terms, and is strongly supported by important political leaders. Of course, strong backing by political leaders in the receiving country is not only of political interest to the United States, but also increases the chances that the project will receive sustained host country support and thereby contribute effectively to growth.

An impact project may be, but is not always, also a pet project. The acceleration of work on the Djakarta By-pass in Indonesia was intended both to have wide public impact and to please a top official. In 1962 the United States was helping to construct a highway to serve the port area of Djakarta and by-pass the congested parts of the city. The project was designed to speed up traffic into and from the port area, and meet economic criteria. President Sukarno approached the American Ambassador and urged that the by-pass be completed by the time of the Asian Games. The highway ran near the site of the Games; the Chinese and the Russians were building a stadium and a hotel for use during the Games, and Sukarno suggested that it would be good publicity if the American-financed highway were also ready for the event. The Ambassador agreed to accelerate construction, despite the substantially increased costs involved—not only increased dollar expenditures, but also friction with the Indonesian officials sharing responsibility for construction.

The token or presence programs in about 20 sub-Saharan African countries, described in Chapter 2, are also justified primarily as demonstrations of U.S. interest. Unlike the other good will techniques, they take the form of a continuing, though modest, aid flow. As a group, they account for much more aid than all the other forms of good will aid together, but even so, they use less than 1 per cent of total A.I.D. funds annually.

The projects that make up these programs meet development criteria: typical examples are secondary-level technical schools, scholarships for study in the United States or in other African nations with more advanced educational institutions, road-building equipment accompanied by several technicians to advise and train in modern construction and maintenance techniques, or modest agricultural projects. Technical assistance has made up most of these programs, but occasional capital projects have been financed. However, the total volume of aid provided—an annual average of $1.2 million per country between 1962 and 1967—has been too small to have a substantial impact on growth.

By 1964, the value of the small African aid programs began to be increasingly critically examined within the Executive Branch, in part because of growing Congressional pressure to reduce the number of countries receiving aid. Though now past history, the debate is still an interesting study of conflicting considerations. Defenders of the presence programs argued that the United States could not afford to be indifferent to events in even the smaller sub-Saharan African countries, despite their small size (the largest has 6.3 million people, and the median population in the group is 3.3 million), their early stage of development, and their lack of trade or historic ties with the United States. Most fundamentally, the people of these countries are a fifth of the population of Africa; their welfare and progress could not be ignored. Nor would other foreign powers be indifferent, regardless of our actions; both the Soviet Union and the Chinese Communists have been quick to exploit political opportunities in these countries.

Although the French, British, and Belgians provide most of the aid and exercise great influence in these countries, their views (particularly French views) diverge from U.S. views on some important issues. Therefore it is important to maintain independent channels of communication and influence. Moreover, leaving the job to others might be self-defeating. The governments of these countries are painfully aware of their continued dependence on their former colonial rulers and are eager to loosen the ties. Assistance from another Free World donor helps to lessen their sense of dependence and may ease pressure to turn to Communist assistance. For all these reasons, supporters of the presence programs concluded that an investment of 1 per cent of total annual economic aid was warranted.

However, views differed within the Executive Branch as to the value of these programs. Critics argued that the limited U.S. goals of demonstrating interest, providing modest development support, and improving diplomatic access could be equally well served through a combination of Peace Corps programs, U.S. regional aid activities such as disease control, scholarship programs, or communications systems, and support for African regional organizations' development programs. Indeed, they suspected that the modest size of the programs and A.I.D.'s complex administrative requirements caused disappointed expectations rather than improved relations. Moreover, they suggested that because many of these countries are so small and resource-poor, channeling aid through regional organizations or projects to promote economic cooperation might be the most effective way to assist their development. The advocates of presence programs replied that whereas Peace Corps and A.I.D.-funded regional activities might have been adequate at the outset, it was quite a different matter to terminate bilateral A.I.D. programs once they had been under way for several years. Termination of aid to all or most of the countries in the group would inevitably be interpreted as a decision to downgrade Africa's priority in U.S. policy, and would have repercussions well beyond the countries involved.

In summer of 1966 the Executive Branch debate over presence programs, which had continued fitfully for several years, was caught up in a broader reconsideration of aid policy in Africa as a whole. That spring President Johnson had requested U.S. Ambassador to Ethiopia Edwin Korry to conduct such a reappraisal. The President was particularly interested in the possibility of channelling more aid through multilateral institutions and directing aid to regional and subregional organizations and projects. The Korry Report, submitted in August, recommended that future bilateral aid to Africa be concentrated in those countries whose size and human and natural resources offered good growth prospects. U.S. aid to other African nations should go primarily through regional and multilateral programs. The Report also stressed the particular importance in Africa of close coordination with other donor nations, and suggested that the World Bank was particularly well suited for this role. President Johnson approved the Korry Report, and A.I.D. plans call for ending bilateral assistance to most of the smaller African countries as soon after July 1967 as current projects can be satisfactorily completed. In some cases this may take several years. Thereafter, aid to these countries will take the form of support for regional institutions, direct financing of regional projects, and participation with other donors in funding major capital projects. However, U.S. Ambassadors in these countries will continue to be authorized to draw on a Self-Help Fund, up to a ceiling of $200,000 annually in each country, to finance small, single-shot projects. Part of these funds might be used in collaboration with Peace Corps activities. Although the new policy grew out of accumulated experience with the special nature of development problems in Africa and the U.S. role as a relatively minor donor in most of the continent, the change was certainly spurred by the Congressional action mentioned earlier, restricting the number of countries outside Latin America for which technical assistance and development loan funds could be used.[40]

The "holding action" programs discussed in Chapter 2—the small programs conducted in Ghana under Nkrumah, Algeria under Ben Bella, Indonesia in the last year or so of Sukarno's rule, British Guiana under Jagan, or wherever the United States is unwilling or unable to cooperate with the existing government but seeks to retain some ties with the population—are also a form of aid motivated primarily by desire to maintain or improve relations with aid recipients. Such programs are usually aimed either at key groups with which the United States seeks to build up contacts, or simply at parts of the public at large. In Algeria, for example, modest A.I.D. and more substantial Food for Peace assistance has concentrated on food-for-work programs to relieve unemployment and on clinics to combat the eye ailments that afflict much of the population. In the period 1963–1966, aid to Ghana consisted almost entirely of limited technical assistance for rural agricultural extension programs.[41] The much-reduced program planned for Indonesia in 1965 was to have emphasized public and business administration training in the United States for army officers and other training programs for key groups.

Holding action programs have two important public relations costs. They are a particular target of Congressional criticism. They also lead friendly and cooperative governments to question the criteria on which the United States extends aid, especially if they themselves are at loggerheads with the countries where the United States conducts such programs. For example, while Nkrumah was in power, Ghana's neighbors found modest but continuing U.S. technical assistance to Ghana irritating and difficult to understand, because

[40] Statement of the Hon. Herman Kleine, Acting Assistant Administrator, Bureau for Africa [A.I.D.], before the House Foreign Affairs Committee, April 20, 1967. Also A.I.D., *Summary Presentation to the Congress, FY 1968,* pp. 201–203, 206.

[41] Large loans to Ghana to support the ambitious Volta River Dam and associated aluminum works were made in 1962 by A.I.D. and the Export-Import Bank. The World Bank also supported the project. The decision was made at a time when cooperation with Nkrumah seemed possible, and when repercussions of refusing to support the Aswan Dam in Egypt were fresh in U.S. officials' minds.

Nkrumah was a disruptive influence in African affairs as well as openly hostile to the United States. Each of these programs, therefore, represents a gamble that the long-run advantages will justify the current costs, monetary and nonmonetary. Sometimes the stakes have not seemed worthwhile: aid to Congo (Brazzaville) was withdrawn when cooperation with that government became too difficult.

The Congo (Brazzaville) case illustrates the final use of aid in connection with general relations between the United States and the recipient nation: aid withdrawn to demonstrate U.S. offense at behavior stretching the elastic limits of diplomatic tolerance too far. More recently, in November 1966, the United States suspended economic aid to Guinea after that country accused the United States of complicity in an incident involving Guinean diplomats passing through Ghana, placed the U.S. Ambassador under house arrest, and expelled the Peace Corps and the United States Information Service from the country. [42] As mentioned earlier, in April 1967 the A.I.D. mission to Yemen was withdrawn after demonstrations and the arrest of two U.S. personnel on an unlikely charge.

Investment, Trade, Base Rights

Aid is used to protect and promote not only good will but also specific U.S. economic and security interests. Written into the Foreign Assistance Act is a provision that assistance shall be withheld from any country that nationalizes or expropriates the property of U.S. citizens without adequate compensation. In June 1962, Ceylon nationalized 63 gasoline stations owned by Esso Standard Eastern, Inc. and Caltex Ceylon, Ltd. After unsuccessful efforts to arrange for compensation to the firms, economic assistance was broken off in February 1963 and was not resumed until July 1965 after the new Senanayake government had come to power and had agreed to compensate the firms.[43]

The case of Peru is less clear-cut but perhaps more interesting. The International Petroleum Corporation (IPC), a wholly-owned subsidiary of Standard Oil of New Jersey with assets of roughly $180 million, had long enjoyed special tax concessions in Peru. For this and other reasons, it was a favorite whipping boy of Peruvian nationalists. When running for the Presidency in 1963, Fernando Belaunde Terry promised to settle the issue, without making clear whether he meant expropriation or renegotiation of the company's

---

[42] *New York Times* November 1, 9, 10, 1966.
[43] *Ibid.*, July 4, 1965.

tax privileges. After his election, a bill was submitted to the Peruvian Congress annulling aspects of the IPC's privileges. As long as Peru did not actually expropriate the firm, the U.S. Executive was not legally required to suspend aid, and could use its discretion as to what measures, if any, were advisable. To discourage passage of the bill and to persuade the Government of Peru to negotiate its differences with IPC, the United States delayed a number of pending loans. Technical assistance, Food for Peace, and military assistance were not affected.[44] In the event, the Peruvian Congress returned the expropriation bill to the Executive, and negotiations were indeed begun, but since have limped along inconclusively. The U.S. action probably helped to discourage expropriation, although it did not bring a satisfactory settlement. However, the costs of this partial success may have been high. The Belaunde regime is regarded as one of the most progressive and promising in Latin America, and it is likely that substantial capital assistance would have been made available were it not for the IPC dispute. A number of U.S. officials had opposed the policy from the start, on the grounds that it was not likely to succeed and was interfering with support to a promising regime; long-run and major U.S. interests in Peru's development were being sacrificed to shorter-run and more limited interests. This view was stated publicly by Senator Robert Kennedy (Democrat, New York) in his tour of Latin America in autumn 1965.[45] The policy of withholding loans was always tacit, and therefore no announcement was made of the decision to abandon it, but early in 1966 A.I.D. approved loans to Peru for agricultural credit, rural electrification, and a development bank. [46]

Aside from the negative threat of withdrawing aid if U.S. property is expropriated without adequate compensation, A.I.D. has a variety of positive programs to promote private U.S. investment abroad. These include an information program (for example, publishing and keeping up to date a "Catalogue of Investment Opportunities and Information," which makes available the results of thousands of investment surveys); sharing the costs of investment surveys with potential U.S. investors (if the investor goes ahead on the basis of the survey, he pays the full cost of the survey; if not, he is reimbursed for half the costs); and several types of guaranty programs to reduce

[44] *Washington Post,* February 11, 1966; *New York Times,* February 10, 1966; *The New Republic,* January 1, 1966.

[45] *New York Times,* February 10, 1966.

[46] A.I.D., *Operations Report,* FY 1966, p. 29.

investment risks. These programs are primarily viewed as ways of increasing the flow of private U.S. resources to the developing countries in order to accelerate their growth, but the benefits are expected to be mutual.

Aid is also used to advance U.S. trade prospects, although this purpose almost never dominates specific aid decisions. Most U.S. economic aid is "tied," that is, with certain exceptions it must be used to purchase U.S. goods and services. This restriction was introduced in stages in the early 1960's, when the U.S. balance of payments, which had been in surplus throughout the 1950's, shifted to a deficit and led to acute concern over the dollar and gold drain. As a result, U.S. aid dollars finance U.S. exports. (However, a recipient nation may simultaneously reduce the quantity of goods purchased from the United States with its "free dollars"—those earned by exports or available through foreign private investment— so that the net increase in U.S. exports to the aid recipient may be less than the full quantity of aid. The proposal that the U.S. insist upon "additionality," mentioned in Chapter 3, would address this problem but would undercut more basic assistance goals.) Aid is also related to U.S. trade interests in the sense that countries that traditionally traded almost exclusively with Europe are becoming acquainted with U.S. goods and services financed by aid, and may come to prefer the United States as a supplier of particular kinds of goods.

Although tying aid is a defensive policy related to balance-of-payments problems rather than to long-run trade interests, and broadened acquaintance with U.S. goods is a by-product of aid undertaken for other purposes, there are two ways in which aid is more deliberately geared to trade promotion. In selecting specific loan projects, A.I.D. officials are instructed to consider among other factors the possibility that the project will generate follow-up orders for U.S. parts and equipment in the future. The importance of this consideration should not be exaggerated. No project would be undertaken primarily because of its potential follow-up orders: the consideration normally would be an additional factor strengthening the case for a project viewed to be desirable on developmental grounds. Second, there have been a few instances where loan proposals have been turned down because they would have helped to finance production of goods which would compete directly with U.S. exports in world markets. In at least one case the private U.S. interests involved brought strong political pressure on the U.S. Government.

There is a strong tendency in Congress and perhaps more widely among the public to want to use aid as a lever to protect other specific economic interests. For instance, in May 1963 two U.S. tuna fishing boats were seized by Ecuador for violating its territorial waters, which it claimed extended 200 miles from shore.[47] This was not the first incident of the kind off Latin American coasts. Senator Thomas Kuchel (Republican, California) introduced and the Senate passed an amendment to the Foreign Assistance Act to bar aid to any nation interfering with U.S. fishing boats in waters the United States regards as international.[48] While the amendment was deleted in conference,[49] more general language was added to later legislation stating the sense of Congress that countries failing to observe international conventions regarding territorial waters should not be eligible for aid.[50]

Economic aid may also be used to maintain base rights. As discussed in Chapter 2, a few years ago more than half a dozen developing countries received substantial economic assistance annually as more or less explicit rental for U.S. military bases or communications centers on their soil. By June 1967, however, all such payments for bases still in use will have been shifted to the budget of the Department of Defense. This will leave one or two country assistance programs where major U.S. military or communications installations lead to substantially greater economic aid than would be made available otherwise, although the aid is not explicit rental and the specific projects financed usually meet developmental criteria.

There is little question as to aid's effectiveness in maintaining access to strategic bases or communications centers. The only questions are whether the gains are worth the direct and indirect costs, and whether economic aid is the most appropriate form of payment. Financing of certain base rights has been transferred to the Department of Defense primarily because Defense is better able than A.I.D. and the Department of State to judge the value of the bases and to weigh this use of funds against alternative uses of defense funds. However, aid has the advantage of serving two goals at once: it maintains access to the base or center, and it promotes economic and social growth. Other forms of payment may also support growth,

[47] *New York Times,* May 29, 1963.
[48] *Ibid.,* November 8, 1963.
[49] *Ibid.,* December 5, 1963.
[50] Foreign Assistance Act of 1965, Section 301(d)(4), adding a new Section 620(o) to the 1961 Act.

but there are no devices built into such payments to encourage developmental uses.

Cold War Attitudes and Roles

To the extent that economic aid promotes good will, it may improve understanding and support for U.S. Cold War policies and views. Aid is also used in more specific ways to buttress Cold War policies and goals.

The Foreign Assistance Act of 1963 prohibits giving economic or military aid to countries whose ships or planes carry strategic goods or "economic assistance" to Cuba; [51] this prohibition has since been extended to cover trade with North Vietnam.[52] Military aid to Spain was frozen in February 1964 because Spanish ships and aircraft continued to trade with Cuba; Greece and Morocco were also temporarily affected. (The Spanish instance illustrates a clear conflict between two shortrun political objectives: preventing Free World trade with Cuba, versus maintaining access to naval bases in Spain for which military aid is the quid pro quo.)[53] The 1966 legislation revising and extending the Food for Peace program introduces a similar restriction on food aid to countries which trade with Cuba and North Vietnam.[54] On occasion the promise of aid has been used as a bribe to induce a country to refuse overflight and landing rights to the Soviet Union (the effort failed), or to indefinitely delay recognition of Communist China (this effort has thus far succeeded). Such efforts are rare; a major and obvious shortcoming is that they are an invitation to blackmail. Yesterday's decision can always be reversed today.

U.S. displeasure over strengthened ties between aid recipients and Communist nations may have been a factor in delaying aid in certain cases. In summer 1965, President Johnson instructed A.I.D. to make no new aid commitments until the appropriations bill then before Congress had been passed. The order was explained in terms of deference to Congress: some Congressmen had complained that A.I.D. sometimes made aid commitments before funds had been appropriated for the current fiscal year. (The appropriations bill

[51] Foreign Assistance Act of 1963, Section 301(e)(1), amending Section 620(a) of the 1961 Act.
[52] Foreign Assistance Act of 1965, Section 301(d)(4), adding a new Section 620(n) to the 1961 Act, and Foreign Assistance Act of 1966, Section 301(h)(4), further strengthening 620(n).
[53] *Christian Science Monitor*, February 29, 1964.
[54] Food for Peace Act of 1966, Section 103(d)(3).

often is not passed until two or three months after the beginning of the year, and A.I.D. normally makes loan commitments amounting to a small fraction of expected appropriations before the funds are actually in hand.) Although aid to several countries was affected by the order, the most immediate and obvious effect was to postpone a scheduled meeting of the Pakistan Consortium at which donors were to pledge aid for Pakistan's development plan. The Administration was known to be upset over Pakistani overtures to Communist China, and this fact was inevitably associated with the aid freeze, causing sharp resentment in Pakistan.[55]

Considerably more important in the context of Cold War politics than such single-shot uses of aid is the effort to prevent excessive reliance on Communist sources of assistance, that is, a degree of reliance that seems likely to lead to internal subversion or foreign policy alignment with the Soviet bloc or Communist China. The U.S. Government does not view any and all Communist aid as politically threatening to the recipient. Substantial Soviet aid to a politically sophisticated country such as India is more likely to be welcomed as additional developmental resources. However, the Communist influx into Zanzibar immediately following its independence, and into Burundi during the height of the Congo crisis, caused deep concern.

Probably the clearest instance of "counter-bloc" assistance in the past few years took place in Guinea. In 1958, when President Charles de Gaulle offered the then-French colonies of sub-Saharan Africa a choice between joining the French community or complete independence, Guinea alone chose the latter course. France then withdrew both the budgetary support and almost all the hundreds of civil servants, technicians, and teachers who, in Guinea as in most of French-speaking Africa, permitted the government and economy to function. Guinea turned in desperation to the Soviet Union, which responded with substantial technical assistance and with loans to be repaid over a number of years by Guinean exports to the Soviet Union. Within a couple of years, Guinea became disillusioned with reliance on the Soviet Union. Soviet technical blunders and Guinea's realization that she had mortgaged her exports undoubtedly contributed to the change of attitude, but the primary cause was interference in Guinean politics by the Soviet Embassy. The Soviet Ambassador was expelled, and Guinea turned to the United States to reduce its reliance on the Soviet Union. The United

States responded with substantial technical, commodity, and project loan assistance. The diplomatic crisis of November 1966 undoubtedly would have caused a reassessment of the U.S. aid program in Guinea, but the concurrent revamping of U.S. aid policy in Africa as a result of the Korry Report led to the decision that U.S. bilateral aid to Guinea, as well as to most other African nations, would be phased out gradually over several years.

The objective of preventing excessive reliance on the Soviet Union continues to be a strong element in U.S. aid to Afghanistan, and figures prominently in several other country programs. In Afghanistan, however, U.S. assistance is considerably smaller than Soviet aid; early Soviet-U.S. rivalry has now evolved into a tacit pattern of semicooperation.

Desire to counter Communist influence and aid must be weighed against other considerations. For example, in summer 1963 the Somali Republic, which has territorial claims in both Ethiopia and Kenya and had clashed repeatedly with Ethiopia on the frontier in the Ogaden region,[56] pressed both the Western powers and the Soviet Union to help her build a larger army. In August the Somali Prime Minister visited Moscow and was offered approximately $30 million to build up an army of 20,000 men. (The Somali army at that time numbered about 4,000). The United States was not willing to counter fully the Soviet offer. To do so would infuriate Ethiopia, where more major interests were at stake; would make the United States party to a sharp escalation of the arms race in the Horn of Africa (in which we were, however, already involved through substantial military aid to Ethiopia); and would also give the United States at least indirect responsibility for an excessive budget burden on a very weak economy. The United States did, however, join with West Germany and Italy to offer Somalia defensive military equipment for an army of 5,000 to 6,000 men, plus engineering equipment, which could be used by the army for internal development projects. The total offer came to a third or a half of the Soviet bid, and was contingent on Somalia's agreeing not to accept arms from any other source. Not surprisingly, Somalia took the higher bid.[57]

Sometimes, the threat is not so much overall economic entanglement as external Communist influence in sensitive fields such as mass media, education, or police. Then an effort may be made to pre-empt such areas for Western (not necessarily U.S.) influence, or

[56] It was not clear which nation had provoked the fighting.
[57] *New York Times,* November 11, December 13, 1963.

at least to counterbalance Communist influence. For example, in Somalia the U.S. has for some years given substantial aid to the Western-oriented police force, in the form of equipment, training, and financing for a police academy. In the context of heavy Soviet assistance to the Somali army, U.S. support for the police takes on a counter-Communist significance.[58] Similarly, U.S. assistance to Indonesia in the last two or three years of Sukarno's control financed management and administration courses at American schools for several hundred Indonesian military officers,[59] and also provided local currency from Food for Peace sales to help finance the army's farm improvement and public works programs.[60] The army was considered the major counterweight to the Indonesian Communist Party.

Where the volume and much of the content of a sizeable aid program has been largely determined by counter-Communist motives, it is fair to test aid's effectiveness in terms of the country's internal political evolution and international alignment, though one must recognize that aid is only one among many factors at work. On this criterion, aid has contributed to a few clear successes, such as Afghanistan, where a consistently neutral foreign policy has been combined with gradual liberalization of a traditional political system. U.S. assistance also made it possible for Guinea to maintain a foreign policy that was independent, albeit more radical in many respects than the United States would prefer, without risking complete economic collapse. There have also been failures, such as Cambodia, where counter-Communist motives played a major role in the substantial aid program terminated at Prince Norodom Sihanouk's request in autumn 1963. In this case Sihanouk's judgment that trends in Southeast Asia favored China rather than the United States undoubtedly was determining—and appropriately so, from his standpoint. It seems fair to conclude that aid cannot persuade a government to pursue a line it does not wish to follow. It can, however, reduce the costs of the country's following the policy it itself prefers. Moreover, where aid can bolster the power and effectiveness of moderate groups within a country, it may influence the outcome of internal debates over the appropriate foreign policy for the country.

[58] Peter Schmid, "Somalia's Instant Army," *The Reporter,* September 24, 1964, p. 50.

[59] This was not military training, which would be financed from military assistance.

[60] *New York Times,* August 21, 1964.

International Cooperation and Peaceful Settlement of Disputes

Aid is also used, apart from Cold War strategies, to encourage peaceful resolution of disputes among developing countries and to support the evolution of effective regional organizations. By law, A.I.D. and Food for Peace assistance are prohibited to any country which the President determines is engaging in or preparing for aggressive military efforts against the United States or U.S.-aided countries.[61]

In an effort to dissuade Indonesia from her confrontation policy toward Malaysia, as well as to register U.S. offense at increasingly strident anti-U.S. statements and actions, aid to Indonesia was drastically curtailed between 1963 and 1965. Substantial commitments had been made in early 1963, when the West Irian problem had just been settled, the Malaysia issue was still over the horizon, and the United States hoped that Sukarno would turn his attention to Indonesia's immense internal development problems. Over $35 million in A.I.D. funds plus $86 million in Food for Peace sales agreements (net of U.S. uses) were provided in 1963. By fiscal 1965, A.I.D. funds had been halted,[62] and food aid had dwindled to only $3 million, financing relief programs run by private charitable organizations.[63]

The 22-day war in 1965 between India and Pakistan over Kashmir caused acute concern and considerable soul-searching in Washington. Both countries were recipients of massive U.S. economic aid. The war was not only directly costly, but also threatened to divert additional resources from development by stimulating an arms race. Moreover, the Indians had long claimed and some U.S. officials agreed that U.S. military assistance to Pakistan gave that country the means to pursue an armed solution to the 18-year-old Kashmir dispute. Former Ambassador to India John Kenneth Galbraith testified before the Senate Foreign Relations Committee that in his judgment, "If we had not supplied arms, Pakistan would not have sought a military solution. That, beyond the slightest possibility of doubt, was the price of the Dulles policy [of arming Pakistan as anchor country in the CENTO and SEATO pacts]." [64]

---

[61] Foreign Assistance Act of 1963, Section 301(e)(3), adding a new Section 620(i) to the 1961 Act.

[62] Technically, the balance for that year is minus $6.3 million, representing deobligation of funds previously committed for now-cancelled projects.

[63] A.I.D., *U.S. Overseas Loans and Grants, 1945–1965*, p. 62.

[64] Selig Harrison, *Washington Post,* June 26, 1966.

Commodity assistance to both countries was suspended during the hostilities. The ban on all but marginal military equipment was continued after both countries agreed to a cease-fire. In April 1967 the U.S. Government announced that it would not resume arms aid to either country, and would withdraw its military advisory and supply groups.[65] Moreover, in mid-1966 a quiet diplomatic effort was made to link long-term economic aid levels to defense budget reductions on both sides of the border. Predictably, the effort was greeted coolly by both countries. India argues that it must maintain an adequate defense against China and cannot scale its military power to Pakistan's fears; Pakistan regards the totality of Indian forces as a threat, and argues that if the United States were willing to use economic aid as leverage on defense budgets, it might also consider using leverage on India to settle the Kashmir dispute. The amount of pressure the United States is prepared to exert on Pakistan is undoubtedly affected by the U.S. interest in maintaining access to security installations there. U.S. diplomatic efforts to limit arms are also undercut by continuing and substantial Chinese arms deliveries to Pakistan. The Soviet position is ambiguous: it has appeared to be torn between its well-established role as India's source of certain military equipment, and desire to follow up on its role as mediator at the Tashkent Conference.[66]

Long predating the 1965 war is U.S. support for the Indus Basin Development Fund. West Pakistan and northwest India share a common river system. Diversion of the water supply has been a perennial source of dispute. The Indus Waters Treaty allocates the waters of certain rivers to India, but Pakistan is to be compensated by construction of works to improve its water supply. The Indus Basin Development Fund, which is administered by the World Bank, was organized to construct these works. Hence U.S. support for the Fund contributes not only to development in both countries, but also to easing friction between them.

In the Middle East, the U.S. interest in preventing open fighting and encouraging stability and moderation has provided the basis for continuing support to Jordan. The UAR presents a more ambiguous and complex case. Since 1962, the United States has sold Egypt roughly $130 million annually (net of U.S. uses) in Food for Peace commodities, mostly wheat, for soft currency on lenient terms.[67]

---

[65] *New York Times,* April 13, 1967.
[66] *Washington Post,* June 26, 1966.
[67] A.I.D., *U.S. Overseas Loans and Grants* 1945–1965, p. 22.

Despite Nasser's periodic acrimonious outbursts to the contrary, the UAR urgently needs the wheat; the Soviet Union finds it difficult to provide large quantities of wheat for use abroad and no other ready sources are at hand. Food aid has been openly and repeatedly used to try to restrain Egyptian involvement in regional affairs—the Arab-Israeli dispute, military intervention in Yemen, political pressures on Jordan and Saudi Arabia, aid to the Congolese rebels—as well as to express U.S. annoyance at symbolic gestures on the part of the UAR such as permitting the Viet Cong to open a Cairo office. Food shipments were suspended for six months in 1965, and were resumed in June after "relations improved," that is, after the UAR halted assistance to the Congolese rebels and moderated its statements on the Arab-Israeli dispute.[68] A year later Food for Peace programs were again suspended in response to renewed UAR propaganda attacks on Saudi Arabia and Israel and U.S. annoyance over the Viet Cong office, as well as U.S. domestic political considerations.[69]

The dispute between Turkey and Greece over Cyprus and the Ethiopian-Somali border conflict in the Ogaden are cases where U.S. arms aid had the unintended though predictable effect of heightening the disposition to resort to arms. On the other side of the ledger, economic and military assistance contributed to good U.S. relations with each country, presumably increasing our ability to exercise a restraining influence. If the United States had given no military assistance, it would be free of any indirect responsibility for the conflicts. However, Greece and Turkey are NATO members and arms aid has been viewed as essential to NATO force goals. Ethiopia is the site of an important communications center; U.S. military assistance is a quid pro quo for the site. The problem is again one of weighing conflicting foreign policy objectives. In some cases it has seemed likely that a country denied arms aid from the United States will seek and obtain it elsewhere. In such circumstances, withholding U.S. aid absolves the United States from responsibility for, but does not prevent, possible subsequent misuse of the arms, while costing the United States some measure of good will and perhaps some influence over the use of the arms. This reasoning entered into the decision, for example, to provide Jordan with certain major military items in 1965 and 1966.

U.S. support for subregional, regional, and international organiza-

[68] *Washington Post,* June 23, 1965.
[69] *Ibid.,* July 31, 1966.

tions as agencies for peaceful resolution of disputes and for cooperation on developmental tasks has been much less ambiguous than the actual (as distinct from intended) U.S. role in disputes among pairs of countries. Through both diplomacy and financial assistance the United States has strongly promoted such organizations.

Annual A.I.D. appropriations include contributions to international organizations and programs, most of which are directed by or affiliated with the United Nations, such as the U.N. Development Program and the U.N. Technical and Economic Program for the Congo. Regional organizations like the Asian and African Development Banks may also receive A.I.D.-financed technical assistance; subscriptions to capital funds require special Congressional authorization. Subregional organizations such as the East African Common Services Organization and the Central American institutions working toward integration have received substantial technical and capital assistance. These organizations are concerned with furthering economic growth; however, by their nature they contribute directly and immediately to the U.S. objective of increased international cooperation, whereas developmental aid to individual countries contributes to that end only via the long indirect route of creating a political and economic climate conducive to cooperation.

A few international programs to which the United States contributes through A.I.D. are directly concerned with peacekeeping. The clearest examples are the U.N. Emergency Force, which until May 1967 patroled and acted as a buffer force on the borders between Israel and its neighbors, and the U.N. peacekeeping operation in Cyprus.

In addition to financing technical and capital support for international and regional organizations, aid has been used on rare occasions to win diplomatic support for such organizations. Probably the clearest example was a $5 million bribe to Haiti, to be used to construct an international airport, in return for Haiti's supporting vote for the Charter of Punta del Este establishing the Alliance for Progress. The Charter vote was expected to be close, and Haiti's vote therefore appeared important.[70] Haiti voted for the Charter. Funds for the airport were later cut off when the entire U.S. aid program to Haiti was suspended at the end of 1962.[71]

[70] Arthur Schlesinger, *One Thousand Days,* Houghton-Mifflin, Boston, 1965, pp. 782–783.
[71] *Washington Post,* January 16, 1966.

Political Uses of Aid: Morality and Effectiveness

This survey suggests the great variety of short-run political uses of aid, and may give some idea of the past effectiveness of aid for particular purposes. At the risk of repetition, it should be underscored that the total amount of aid used for all such purposes is a small fraction of A.I.D. activities: the great bulk of U.S. economic aid is used to promote development (about 65 per cent) or to combat immediate and continuing security problems (until 1967, 20 to 25 per cent).

The use of aid for immediate political purposes is criticized on four counts: that such uses are immoral; that they often conflict with more permanent and important interests and therefore are ill-advised; that aid is usually an ineffective instrument for short-run political goals; and that such uses of aid are costly in terms of Congressional and public relations in the United States and abroad.

Morality

The long-established U.S. principle of nonintervention leads many Americans to view efforts to influence another country's internal political situation as immoral, regardless of the means. A separate strand of criticism on moral grounds concerns means rather than ends: although most Americans would applaud the goal of assuring approval of the Charter of Punta del Este, many might condemn the use of bribery as means. Suspicion regarding goals as well as distaste for means colors the language of the Republican Citizens' Committee report quoted at the beginning of this chapter: " . . . the use of aid for short-run political purposes . . . a kind of bribe or bludgeon to accomplish any and all kinds of U.S. foreign policy purposes."

American attitudes toward attempts to influence the internal political situation in another country are curiously inconsistent. Many persons feel that trying to influence the outcome of elections is immoral. Most might question exertion of direct pressure to change the composition of the government, as in the case of Laos. But most Americans applaud the policy of withdrawing aid from military juntas that have taken power by force. Senator Morse, who has been a particularly caustic critic of short-run aid, publicly and strongly advocated this response in autumn 1963 after coups had occurred in the Dominican Republic and Honduras within a ten-day period.[72] And most persons probably would not view as immoral the goal of sustaining a new constitutional regime until it has had a chance to organize its program and policies. Yet pressure on juntas and support for new regimes are both forms of intervention.

The kind of intervention in other nations' politics which is probably morally acceptable to most Americans is that intended to permit internal political processes to proceed in an orderly and constitutional manner—such as actions to remove the threat of collapse due to temporary financial crisis, to relieve unemployment among key groups or in key areas, to suppress terrorist attempts to sabotage elections, to discourage military intervention in politics. U.S. action taken to influence the *outcome* of political processes is viewed as much more questionable. In principle many persons even in the developing countries might find this formulation acceptable, but in practice the distinction is hard to draw. The principal actors in a nation's political affairs understandably might view as intervention an action the United States regarded as an effort to permit orderly procedure. The strongest defense for U.S. efforts to influence directly the outcome of political processes is pragmatic: in some circumstances, if immediate events go wrong, the future may be forfeited for many years. This argument is probably used too frequently, but it is sometimes valid.

The clearest instance of a political use of aid which is widely viewed as an immoral *means* of conducting foreign policy, regardless of the validity of the objective sought, is outright bribery—the explicit offer of assistance in return for specific host country action. As Professor Morgenthau has observed, "Bribes offered by one government to another for political advantage were until the beginning of the nineteenth century an integral part of the armory of diplomacy. No statesman hesitated to acknowledge the giving and accepting of bribes." [73] Morgenthau attributes the current reluctance to admit the use of bribery to "a climate of opinion which accepts as universally valid the proposition that the highly developed industrial nations have an obligation to transfer money and services to underdeveloped nations for the purpose of economic development." [74] I am more inclined to account for distaste for bribery in the international realm as an extension of nineteenth- and twentieth-century attitudes toward

[72] *Washington Post,* October 4, 1963.
[73] Morgenthau, *op. cit.,* p. 302.
[74] *Ibid.*

bribery in domestic politics, business, and public administration. If this is correct, it is fair to note that international politics is less structured and incorporates much less agreement on guiding principles than is true of domestic politics or business in the developed countries; therefore, to apply the same moral criteria to the different realms may be unrealistic. In any event, outright bribery plays a very minor role even in that fraction of total aid activities directly aimed at political goals. A much greater part of political aid is more accurately described as the effort to create a climate in which the recipient country will behave as the United States prefers—that is, one in which internal political processes can proceed in an orderly manner, good will toward the United States prevails regardless of possible disagreements on specific issues, and excessive reliance on Communist aid and consequent subservience to Communist desires are unnecessary.

The morality of withholding food aid as a means of accomplishing political goals might also be questioned. Where the goal is adoption of better economic policies, perhaps the means can be justified by the benevolent intention. This was a major element in the temporary U.S. delay in grain shipments to India in autumn 1966. Though severe drought threatened in early 1967, and limited port capacity meant that a break in shipments would risk a corresponding drop in daily grain rations in drought regions, it had been evident for a long time that basic reforms in Indian agricultural policy were essential for long-run progress. Even so, the timing of the pressure could be questioned on moral grounds. Where the objective in withholding food aid is not to press for better development policies but to influence a nation's foreign policy (as in the case of the UAR) or to serve other goals of interest primarily to the United States, the question becomes still more doubtful. The issue arises, of course, only where the country's own food supplies are extremely low.

Priority

A second major criticism of the use of aid for immediate political goals rests on the judgment that such goals are often low-priority or ephemeral, and conflict with more lasting and important objectives. Some political goals, such as preventing trade between Cuba and other developing countries, or excluding Communist China from the United Nations, are criticized as self-defeating. Delaying capital assistance to Peru in an effort to promote a settlement with the International Petroleum Company was a classic case of sacrificing major long-term interests to less important short-run goals. More generally, use of some aid for political purposes tends to undermine the policy of linking the bulk of development aid to improved self-help efforts in aid-receiving nations. For example, repeated emergency assistance to bolster and keep the friendship of an inept regime may lead neighboring countries to question how seriously the United States means its oft-proclaimed self-help criteria. Such "disincentive effects" are rarely taken into account in deciding to extend crisis assistance. However, although short-run political aid may often conflict with longer-run objectives, some short-run goals are extremely important precisely because they affect subsequent options. This was true of approval of the Charter of Punta del Este, the holding of elections in Venezuela, and the outcome of elections in Chile.

Effectiveness

The argument that aid is not an effective instrument for short-run security and political purposes, like the arguments regarding morality and priority, turns out to be true for some attempted uses of aid and patently false for others. Base buying is obviously effective; the aid achieves its stated purpose. The decision to switch payments for bases to the budget of the Department of Defense reflected considerations of internal U.S. Government budgetary and decision-making convenience, not a judgment that aid was not serving the purpose adequately. To take a more interesting category, aid has proved helpful in giving new regimes a breathing space in which to formulate their programs. The programs themselves have not always been effective; however, solving problems is much more difficult than providing time in which to formulate solutions. Without time for analysis, the chances of good solutions are reduced. Most U.S. Ambassadors to the African countries receiving presence programs agree that the programs give them much better diplomatic access than they would otherwise enjoy. The effectiveness of the programs in promoting good will is much less clear. The clause denying aid to countries that expropriate U.S. property has probably helped to discourage such moves. The ban on aid to countries that permit trade with Cuba and North Vietnam has shut off a trickle of trade but has had little real effect, because neither the Communist nor the industrialized non-Communist nations, which are Cuba's largest actual and potential trading partners, are affected by the ban. Aid's impact on the outcome of particular elections has probably been marginal (whether the elections produced the U.S.-preferred result or not), but there are one or two cases where its contribution may have been significant (surely not determining). The scorecard on providing alternatives to excessive dependence on Communist sources of aid, and countering external Communist influence in specific important fields is somewhat better.

Aid is less likely to be effective in pursuing political objectives when it is used on a "crash" basis, without careful consideration of the chances of success in the particular situation. The more successful political uses of aid are often not crisis measures, but activities and programs designed to address a continuing political problem over a period of time. Analysis of the problem and consideration of how to cope with it then becomes a part of the regular program planning process for the country concerned.

A.I.D.'s efforts to adhere to development criteria reduce aid's effectiveness for many immediate political uses. Professor Hans Morgenthau has noted that aid for "prestige" and "bribery" purposes has been represented as development aid to ourselves as well as to the recipient, thereby introducing irrelevant administrative complications.[75] Maintaining development criteria for projects requires time-consuming studies and reviews, which slow down the flow of aid. Moreover, a forest of legal and administrative regulations and restrictions, some imposed for reasons that do not relate to any purposes of aid (such as tying procurement to U.S. goods and services to protect the U.S. balance of payments, or requiring that at least half of the shipping charges associated with any A.I.D. project go to U.S. carriers), complicates and delays aid programs. U.S. Ambassadors and State Department officers in Washington are often exasperated by A.I.D.'s unwillingness or inability to respond to immediate pressures. For example, former Ambassador to Panama Joseph S. Farland aired disputes with A.I.D. when he resigned in August 1963. His major grievance was that A.I.D. exerted too much control over the use of U.S. money. He had favored a sharp speed-up of expenditures for impact projects and elimination of time-consuming surveys and feasibility studies.[76] Many Ambassadors in smaller African countries are convinced that insistence on development standards, as well as administrative and legal restrictions, greatly reduces the usefulness of modest U.S. aid programs in promoting good will.

[75] *Ibid.*, pp. 302–304.
[76] *Washington Post,* September 10, 1963.

Public Relations Costs

The fourth and final charge directed against political uses of aid is that such uses, even when legitimate and effective, jeopardize public and Congressional understanding and support for the foreign assistance effort and tarnish its image abroad. Much of the criticism of foreign aid concerns the number of countries aided and the diffuse nature of aid goals. We have seen that roughly half of all country assistance programs are intended primarily to serve limited (though not necessarily unimportant) political ends. Eliminating some or all of these programs would certainly result in a consolidated, neater effort, although it would not reduce the aid bill significantly. Similarly, elimination of short-run political elements in primarily developmental country programs would simplify the explanation to Congress of the volume and content of aid proposed for such programs.

But it is not clear that freeing the assistance effort from short-run political objectives, even were it feasible, would in fact increase support for foreign aid. There is no public and Congressional consensus on what purposes aid should serve and what goals should be eliminated. Congress has directed that development aid be used for development purposes. Yet it has also imposed an ever-lengthening list of restrictions and prohibitions on the use of aid, such as bans on aid to countries that trade with Cuba and North Viet Nam, that expropriate U.S. property, or that fail to observe international conventions affecting fishing interests. Although they deplore "good will" aid, Congressmen are deeply disturbed by anti-U.S. statements by or demonstrations in countries that receive U.S. assistance of any kind. It is, of course, less expensive to withhold aid for political reasons than to give it for such purposes. However, the principle is much the same.

The public relations costs of political uses of aid are more clear-cut in the developing countries themselves. Those concerned with the threat of neocolonialism see evidence that the program is at bottom neocolonialist in the fact that most aid is tied to purchase of U.S. goods and services, in the effort to exert influence on recipients' development policies, and in the use of aid to protect and promote U.S. investments. Those who suspect political intervention can find instances where aid has been used to intervene. Those who view the United States as an aggressive militarist power can point to the use of aid to maintain base rights. Nondevelopmental aid, and regulations regarding the administration of development aid, cloud the image of generous, "no-strings-attached" support for mutually beneficial growth.

It has been repeatedly suggested that many of these problems could be avoided by giving the Department of State a "slush fund" for political purposes. This would avoid confusion with economic aid and consequent erosion of the credibility of development criteria. Such a fund would also—if Congress so designed it—be free from exasperating and irrelevant economic and administrative criteria. Despite these advantages, the slush fund idea has serious drawbacks. If the fund were large enough to deal with major crises and problems, Congress almost certainly would impose controls on its use similar to current provisions governing the use of Supporting Assistance—which, after all, is designed to serve such purposes. Moreover, many crises have important economic as well as political dimensions, and their solutions have implications for future development; it would be unfortunate in such cases to divorce crisis action from current or potential development assistance. Third, a clearly labeled slush fund would be ineffective where the United States or (perhaps more often) the recipient government prefers to maintain the appearance of "respectable" economic aid. Finally, the Self-help Fund in most aided countries can now finance a wide variety of small projects with a minimum of red tape, meeting the need for a flexible instrument available for uses where more elaborate review and control are not warranted.

Desire for an instrument more responsive to immediate political pressures has occasionally led to more drastic proposals. In early 1964, Undersecretary of State George W. Ball, chairing a committee appointed by the President to review foreign aid, pressed hard for the dismantling of A.I.D. and the assignment of responsibility for a severely trimmed aid program to the Department of State.[77] The proposal, of course, roused strong resistance, and the President decided against major changes in aid administration.[78]

Aid's limitations as a political instrument could also point to a different, almost opposite conclusion—that instead of seeking to make aid more responsive to immediate political requirements, more imaginative and vigorous use should be made for these purposes of other instruments of U.S. foreign policy. It may well be that the possibility of using aid for short-run goals deters Embassies from explor-

[77] *New York Times,* January 4, 1964.
[78] *Ibid.,* January 17, 1964.

ing less obvious alternatives, including the whole arsenal of traditional diplomatic techniques.

Neither State Department desire for firmer control over the aid program, nor A.I.D. yearning for a "pure" economic assistance program is likely to be resolved. If aid is to serve predominantly developmental goals, semi-independent administration is essential. If it is to be closely integrated with other elements of U.S. foreign policy, it is inevitable that some aid will be used for immediate political purposes. None of the four lines of criticism examined leads to the conclusion that short-run political uses of economic aid should be— or could be—eliminated. All of them, however, suggest the need for considerably more discriminating use of the aid instrument. Sometimes the odds are so clearly against successful use of aid that the effort is unwise despite the importance of the goal. However, probably the greatest abuse is not ignoring the chances of failure in narrow terms but neglecting to consider the impact of political uses on higher-priority goals.

CHAPTER 6

Using Aid to Promote Long-Run Political Development*

THE FOREIGN ASSISTANCE ACT of 1961 called for an "historic demonstration that economic growth and political democracy can go hand in hand. . . ." The function of the economic assistance program that the Act established was, in short, to promote political as well as economic development.

Yet political development has been declared "the missing dimension in American policy toward the developing nations." [1] Little aid activity is directly addressed to political development objectives. In the elaborate process of program planning, the actual and potential impact of assistance on political development receives virtually no attention.

The past two years have seen increasing criticism of the aid program on this score. The Foreign Assistance Act of 1966 added several provisions to the basic foreign aid legislation designed to spur increased political development efforts. Before examining proposals for more vigorous action, however, it is useful to consider what is meant by political development, the pattern of past A.I.D. efforts, and the reasons for the relative neglect of political development.

Political Development, Democratic Evolution, and Economic Growth

An adequate definition of political development has been the topic of innumerable scholarly conferences and articles for more than a decade. It is less difficult to identify major aspects of governmental

---

* This chapter draws on Eugene B. Mihaly and Joan Nelson, "Political Development and U.S. Economic Assistance," paper delivered at the 1966 annual meeting of the American Political Science Association.

[1] Speech by the Hon. Donald M. Fraser, U.S. Congress, reprinted in the *Congressional Record,* July 13, 1966, p. 14765.

and political development that the United States seeks to promote. These include:

1. Administrative competence: reasonably efficient and honest administration, capable of maintaining civil peace and carrying out service and developmental functions.
2. National integration: growing identification with the nation rather than with local, regional, ethnic, religious, or tribal loyalties.
3. More equitable distribution of wealth, income, services, and opportunity among classes, regions, and ethnic groups and between rural and urban areas.
4. Fundamental civil liberties: observance of due process, freedom from arbitrary arrest, freedom of association, occupation, and movement.
5. Provision for the orderly transfer of political power.
6. Development of democratic institutions, that is, those which promote broad participation in government decision making and popular review and sanction of government performance. This in turn requires provision for wide dissemination and exchange of information; tolerance of nonviolent expression of individual and group opinion, including freedom of dissent; encouragement of responsible and effective voluntary associations and interest groups; and often, though not always, decentralization of authority to local (and sometimes regional) government.

Political development is, then, a broader concept than democratic evolution. Not all aspects of political development are uniquely or even necessarily associated with democracy.

Administrative efficiency plainly is compatible with authoritarian and totalitarian regimes: indeed, such governments are often defended in the developing countries because they claim to be more efficient than democratic regimes. National integration has been achieved—and not achieved—under all three forms of government, although conflict is normally more rapidly suppressed and hidden under totalitarianism. All forms of government may act to increase equity, and all have also perpetuated old and created new inequities. Basic civil liberties can be preserved under authoritarian but not under totalitarian systems.

Broad participation in governmental decision making, including popular review and sanction of governmental authority, is the aspect of political development most closely associated with democratic evolution. Policy makers have long faced the dilemma of formulating the appropriate U.S. policy toward a regime that is efficient, concerned for equity and growth, and reasonably respectful of civil liberties, but has sharply curtailed democratic rights and institutions —for example, the early years of President Ayub Khan's regime in Pakistan, the military junta that took over Ecuador in 1963, or the Branco government in Brazil. The United States has usually supported such regimes, while indicating its concern over suppression of democratic processes.

American public and academic acceptance of this course is growing. A decade ago, both military regimes and one-party systems were rejected on principle both by the interested public and by most political scientists. The public is now more tolerant of one-party systems, although antipathy for military regimes seems little affected by such cases as Ayub's Pakistan and the progressive junta in Ecuador. Most scholars now clearly dissociate the broader concept of political development from the specific connotations of parliamentary democracy. Many argue that other aspects of political development are prerequisite to (though no guarantee of) later democratic evolution; therefore, these aspects must take priority over development of democratic institutions.

It would be convenient to assume that political development and economic growth support each other. Indeed, much of the rationale for development aid rests on the assumption that economic stagnation, in the context of rising expectations, population growth, and political agitation, is virtually a formula for instability and extremism. More positively, economic growth is expected in the long run to help unify disparate regions, relieve class tensions, and create groups with a progressive but moderate outlook, in particular an entrepreneurial middle class and a landed peasantry. Conversely, aspects of political development, such as self-help efforts and initiatives of voluntary associations and interest groups, are expected to accelerate economic growth.

Yet the relationship between economic and political development is not always mutually beneficial. Rapid economic growth displaces whole social classes and threatens vested interests, often generating political crises. The increased mobility associated with economic growth can heighten ethnic, religious, or regional tensions by throwing hostile groups into close contact and competition. For example, resentment between Eastern Ibos and Northern Hausa tribesmen in

Nigeria exploded into bloody rioting and massacres in 1966. Traditional tribal enmity had been exacerbated by Ibo control of professional and technical positions and a good deal of business in the North.

Some aspects of political development are essential for economic growth; others are compatible with growth but are not prerequisites; still others have an ambiguous impact. Civil peace and administrative competence plainly promote economic progress. A degree of national integration is also essential, because unchecked rivalries can bring political chaos and economic slowdown or collapse, as in the Congo in the years immediately after independence. Even where there is no threat of widespread violence or secession, ethnic or regional loyalties can interfere with economic growth by distorting resource allocation —for example, by influencing the location of a steel mill or a university, or by creating pressures leading to ethnic or regional quotas in the civil service or in scholarship awards.

The relationship between equity and economic growth is less clear-cut. In most developing countries, broadened services and opportunities including housing, health care, and primary education require heavy initial investment and high recurring costs. Such services contribute only indirectly and in the long run to accelerated economic growth. Other uses of the same funds could promote growth more rapidly and directly. And upon growth depends future capacity to provide employment, higher standards of services, and greater opportunities for the population as a whole. Similarly, whereas privileged groups can and should bear more of the tax burden, investment incentives must not be destroyed. Land reform often results in reduced agricultural production, at least initially. In these and other ways, measures to increase equity may conflict with the requirements of economic growth.

On the other hand, many steps to increase equity promptly and directly are compatible with or even essential to economic progress. Improvements in certain services, notably education and health, contribute not only to well-being but also to productivity. The prospect of a greater share in income or the possibility of owning one's own house normally stimulates initiative and effort. Moreover, many measures to increase equity require little or no increased expenditures, for instance, reduced discrimination between classes or ethnic groups in law enforcement. Some measures, such as stricter tax administration, may even increase revenues as well as equity.

Fundamental civil liberties are compatible with and conducive to economic growth. Controls on movement and occupation are usually costly to administer as well as demoralizing, while arbitrary arrest and lack of due process probably inhibit growth by stifling initiative. But progress in the Soviet Union and several of the East European nations demonstrates that restrictions on such liberties need not prevent growth.

The development of democratic institutions that promote broad participation in governmental decision making has a complex and ambiguous relationship to economic growth. Political participation is sometimes confused with widespread participation in developmental programs. Mobilizing an ever-growing part of the population to take part in and support development programs is an intrinsic and essential aspect of effective economic growth. Economic participation may be stimulated by and channelled through a great variety of organizations, including village self-help associations, cooperatives, labor unions, and other voluntary associations, as well as through vigorous private enterprise. Americans tend to associate cooperatives, labor unions, and other voluntary organizations with democratic forms of government. However, authoritarian and totalitarian regimes also recognize the value of such institutions as a means of mobilizing participation in development programs. Indeed, one of the hallmarks of modern totalitarianism is a proliferation of associations of all kinds to this end—not, of course, as vehicles for independent political initiative and pressure.

Although widespread participation in development efforts clearly promotes economic growth, broadened participation in public policy formulation may or may not do so. At the local level, decentralized decision making has immense advantages of speed and relevance to local conditions. Moreover, an effective voice in local decisions may often stimulate local self-help efforts. Striking progress has been made in the past few years in East Pakistan, where local councils have been given clear responsibility for selecting, designing, executing, and evaluating local projects, along with funds and access to the technical advice required to do so successfully. But it is risky to conclude that increased authority at local levels will automatically promote progress. Local politicians are often both more venal and more traditional in their outlook than national political leaders. If local decision making is dominated by a traditional and conservative local elite or by irresponsible local politicians, increased local authority may impede both economic and political progress.

Active popular participation in and pressure on national decision making also may promote or impede measures essential for long-run growth. Where political power is tightly held by conservative vested interests, broadened political participation in choice of leaders and determination of policies at the national level is a necessary condition for progress. But policies designed to stimulate growth and increase welfare in the long run may call for belt-tightening, deferred claims to increased equity, or temporary suppression of nationalist pride. Higher taxes, lower government subsidies for food or gasoline, postponement of the expansion of elementary schools in order to concentrate on improved quality of secondary education, deferment of massive low-cost housing projects, measures to attract foreign private investment—all are predictably unpopular, yet often necessary. Argentina under Peron and since his ouster offers what may be the most striking illustration of irresponsible public pressure on and participation in national policy: a once-booming and relatively highly developed economy has stagnated. Partly for this reason, many leaders in the developing countries regard democratic rights and processes as luxuries their countries cannot yet afford.

The aspects of political development that most Americans would view as central—increased equity and broadened participation in governmental decision making—thus turn out to be the aspects that relate somewhat ambiguously to economic growth. Other aspects of political development—administrative competence, national integration, and fundamental civil liberties—while more clearly compatible with or essential for economic progress—tend to appear less important to Americans. This may be because we take for granted a relatively high degree of efficiency, unity, and civil liberty, and fail to recognize that absence of these qualities may make a political system as inadequate as marked inequity or restricted participation.

The Pattern of A.I.D. Political Development Efforts

The pattern of U.S. political development efforts can be explained partly in terms of the relations between different aspects of political development and economic growth. A second major factor is the degree of host country sensitivity associated with each facet of political development. To pursue those aspects which clearly promote economic growth and are in principle acceptable to the developing countries themselves creates no conflict of objectives and little diplomatic risk for the United States. Other aspects of political development involve more complicated diplomatic and technical considerations.

Because administrative competence and ability to maintain civil peace are prerequisites for economic growth and the developing countries themselves are eager to develop such competence, A.I.D. provides public administration training and advisors in most of its country programs. Sometimes leverage has been used to press for key administrative reforms. Aid to increase administrative competence is noncontroversial, and the problems of morality and risk discussed later in this chapter do not really apply to it. However, efforts to improve administrative capacity may often have been too narrowly conceived. For example, only recently has A.I.D. begun a few experimental projects to give lawyers a broader grasp of development problems, so that they will use their immense influence in drafting and interpreting laws and regulations to promote growth.

As described in Chapter 2, A.I.D. programs have deliberately attacked the problem of national integration in a few countries where particular isolated and disaffected regions appear to pose an immediate threat of extremism and insurgency—Northeast Thailand, Northeast Brazil, the Peruvian high plateau. Where the problem does not appear as pressing, there has been little deliberate effort to consider ways to promote integration. Transportation projects—for example, roads in Bolivia, and airfields, roads, and bridges in Ethiopia— probably contribute to political integration as well as to economic progress, but the long-run political contribution of the projects has usually been a secondary and almost always a nonoperational consideration. That is, it has had no effect on the design of the project. Long before the bloody tribal clashes of 1966, it was clear that national integration is Nigeria's most fundamental problem. Although the U.S. aid program in Nigeria did include large-scale educational and agricultural projects in the North to help to narrow the disparity between that region and the more advanced South, such efforts were a minor theme in the overall aid effort. This is not to suggest that A.I.D. or any external action could have prevented the eruption of tribal hostilities, but merely to comment on failure to consider adequately a problem of the greatest importance.

Partly because increased equity coincides with many aspects of economic growth, it is tempting to list many of A.I.D.'s activities as contributing to that goal. Expanded education and health services in poorer urban neighborhoods and rural areas, low-cost housing projects, potable water and sewerage projects all improve the services and facilities available to less privileged groups. Stricter tax collection, revised tax structure, and land reform play directly on the distribution of income and wealth. Technical and capital assistance for cooperatives, labor unions, and credit associations may increase the economic and political power of previously unorganized and ineffective groups.

However, A.I.D., like the developing countries themselves, must constantly seek a balance between efforts to increase immediately the income, services, and opportunities of the least privileged, and measures which will best accelerate growth. For example, there have been ardent disputes within A.I.D. over whether to concentrate agricultural assistance in particular countries on more "modern" (cash, sometimes export) crops or types of farms or regions producing such crops, or alternatively to focus on the much larger group of "traditional" farmers who are more difficult to reach and more resistant to change, but whose needs are far greater.

A.I.D. has done little to foster civil liberties. This may reflect the dual judgment that intervention in this sphere is likely to be resented, and that improved observance of such liberties is not of first importance for economic growth. Police training in many countries does stress respect for civil liberties, although police made more efficient through U.S. training and equipment may be and have sometimes been used to support repressive regimes. Improved legal education and better organization and availability of legal reference material may promote this aspect of political development, as well as help lawyers to contribute more effectively to economic growth and administrative efficacy. A.I.D. is currently assisting legal education in Tanzania, Ethiopia, Brazil, and Central America.

The United States makes a greater effort to contribute, directly or indirectly, to development of democratic institutions and to broader and more responsible public participation in governmental decision making. Most of the activities clearly addressed to this goal take the form of attempts to broaden the understanding and influence the attitudes of key groups. The most obvious examples are the labor leadership training programs conducted in Latin America through the AFL-CIO-sponsored American Institute for Free Labor Development, and similar programs in several countries in Africa and Asia. These combine training union leaders for effective union organization and operation—such as instruction in administration, accounting, and arbitration skills—with political indoctrination, which varies from country to country in intensity and approach. One reason for the large number of labor training programs is strong support from U.S. unions which, concerned over leftist influence in union movements abroad, have contributed their own funds and urged broader U.S. Government programs to combat such trends.[2]

Aside from the labor leadership programs, efforts to influence key groups' attitudes are rather scattered. Small groups of political leaders have been brought for observation tours of U.S. political institutions. For example, five high-ranking Kenyan political leaders were brought to the United States in August and September 1964; they observed the Democratic National Convention, took a course on American Government at Syracuse University, and toured polling places in Vermont during primary elections.[3] Groups of young Central American leaders from various fields—teaching, labor, business, administration, and politics—are invited to a continuing series of seminars offered by Loyola University, which feature no-holds-barred discussions of problems of development, including political development. The League of Women Voters, with A.I.D. support, annually selects and trains a small number of Latin American women in techniques of organizing civic groups. In Colombia in summer 1965, the U.S. Ambassador and the A.I.D. Mission Director brought together 35 leading Colombians from business, government, education, and journalism to discuss problems of agricultural development and land reform at a three-day retreat. Military training programs financed from military assistance often include formal or informal discussion of the appropriate role of the military in political affairs.

Some short-term actions, such as withholding aid to demonstrate disapproval of a coup or helping to ensure that elections are held in an orderly atmosphere, are expected not only to gain their immediate goals but also to contribute to long-run respect for and faith in democratic processes. For example, the successful elections and transfer of power in Venezuela in 1963, to which A.I.D. assistance made a modest contribution, probably greatly strengthened Venezuelan confidence in democracy, and may have heartened democratic forces in other Latin American countries.

The promotion of cooperatives, credit unions, peasant federations, and a variety of other associations is a less direct way of strengthening democratic processes. The primary motive for assisting such

---

[2] See series of articles in the *Washington Post* on "Labor's Cold Warrior," starting December 30, 1965.

[3] *Free Press,* Burlington, Vermont, September 9, 1964.

groups usually is to encourage more active and effective participation in economic activity. Farmers' cooperatives make it possible to obtain credit, purchase equipment, and market crops on better terms than individual farmers could obtain. Credit unions mobilize middle-class savings and investment. The U.S. National Farmers' Union, with A.I.D. financing, has selected and trained several hundred rural leaders from several Latin American countries. A.I.D. planners hope and expect that in addition to promoting economic growth, such organizations and individuals, by providing leadership and experience in making group decisions, will create capacity for responsible participation in broader public policy realms.

A.I.D. also provides extensive assistance for education. Most A.I.D. officials believe that better education for more of the population eventually will lead to broader and more responsible participation in public policy formulation. However, the education programs are designed primarily to serve economic and manpower requirements. The expected contribution to political development is a by-product. While A.I.D. provides extensive technical assistance and finances buildings and equipment for university departments directly related to economic growth—engineering, agriculture, veterinary medicine, education, economics, business administration, even home economics—little effort has been made to improve the quality of the non-economic social sciences and law faculties. Yet both political science and law are recruiting grounds for politics and the civil service. Similarly, at the secondary level, A.I.D. has stressed mathematics and science as essential background for training in technical and engineering skills. Civics, history, and social science in general have had low priority.

A.I.D. planners might thus identify an impressive number and variety of specific activities as contributing to one or more political development objectives. The goals of increased administrative competence, greater equity, and broadened political participation in particular seem well addressed. Yet this impression is misleading. The effectiveness of aid efforts depends not only on the number and variety of projects addressed to a problem, but on their coherence and relevance. In most of its fields of activity, A.I.D. does attempt (albeit inadequately) to assess the nature of the problem and to tailor the pattern of activities to individual country circumstances. But A.I.D. political development efforts rarely are based on such analysis, nor do they form coherent, planned programs. When political considerations are seriously analyzed, it is usually in terms of barriers to economic progress. With few exceptions, A.I.D. does not attempt to establish operational political development objectives and to devise an integrated strategy for achieving them. A.I.D. political development efforts therefore are collections of disparate activities, mostly selected and designed with economic and technical criteria in mind. If they form a pattern with respect to political development at all, it is largely by accident.

Nor does A.I.D. seek to anticipate the effect upon political evolution of programs undertaken for economic reasons. Yet such effects may be as or more important than the impact of explicit political development efforts. For example, the network of roads financed by U.S. aid in Turkey in the 1950's, though motivated by economic objectives, almost certainly has contributed powerfully to the political activation of Turkish villagers throughout the nation, and thereby to far-reaching changes in politics and the party system.

U.S. aid programs to Latin America may have a more pronounced political development dimension than programs elsewhere. This is partly due to the political and social goals of the Alliance for Progress and partly because of a retrospective analysis of what went wrong in Cuba. The Charter of Punta del Este provides a multilateral framework for U.S. aid planning with each Latin American country and records a consensus on broad goals, including political development goals. This consensus has some effect even on those governments which are not enthusiastic about the values of the Charter. Experience in Cuba is widely held to be a lesson that economic growth is not enough.

In addition, administrative organization in Washington may encourage more systematic attention to Latin American political development. The State Department's Bureau of Inter-American Affairs and A.I.D.'s Latin America Bureau are merged, with joint staffing of each country desk. This arrangement is not used for any other region. However, it is difficult to sort out the effects of this organizational structure from the other special reasons for more adequate attention to problems of political development in Latin America.

In short, with the partial exception of Latin American programs, A.I.D. acts as if it believed that if it takes care of economic development, political development will take care of itself.

There are several reasons for this economic outlook. First, most A.I.D. officials (and many State Department officers) believe that efforts to affect political development are diplomatically risky. Not only may such efforts jeopardize U.S. relations with the country, but they may defeat their purpose by compromising the groups or institutions we seek to support. Moreover, political development efforts that backfire might undermine U.S. ability to encourage better economic policies.

Second, most A.I.D. officials are skeptical about the efficacy of deliberate efforts, direct or indirect, to shape political evolution. Political development is at least as complex as economic development, but theory about political development is embryonic. Despite the inadequacies of current theory regarding economic development, far more is known than on the political side. Data on political attitudes, values, and patterns of behavior, and how these are related to economic and social variables which A.I.D. activities might affect, are also extremely sparse.

Moreover, A.I.D.'s potential influence in the realm of political development is limited. We have seen that influence and occasional leverage are tools for promoting economic growth as powerful as are direct contributions of skills and capital. But governments are likely to be much less receptive to advice and pressure regarding national integration, the extent and nature of popular participation, the role of interest groups, and the like, than to foreigners' suggestions regarding import control systems or power rates. While even fairly narrow economic policies may have important political repercussions, they appear to be more technical and neutral, hence more appropriate subjects for external intervention. In view of inadequate theory and data and constraints on influence, many Administration officials conclude that they should concentrate their efforts on the task they feel better equipped to handle—economic growth.

A third reason for reluctance to become involved in political development efforts is probably doubt regarding the morality of deliberate efforts to influence another country's political evolution. Moreover, many foreign aid officials probably view with distaste direct or indirect involvement with politics or politicians. A.I.D. staff are primarily technicians, with a sprinkling of economists and programmers. Both the scope of their work and their professional temperament tend to limit their contacts to host country executive agencies. There is more than a touch of the technocratic outlook that politics is an unfortunate and perhaps even unnecessary hindrance to the constructive work of development.

These arguments carry some weight, but do not make a persuasive case against any and all deliberate attempts to promote political development. To argue that it is immoral to attempt to influence another country's political evolution is to set up a false dilemma.

In any sizeable and continuing program, the United States cannot choose *not* to exert political influence. Regardless of U.S. intent, the volume, content, and administration of U.S. aid will in some measure fortify or undermine the distribution of political power and affect the content of political pressures and the extent of political participation. Deliberate intervention, therefore, is not an alternative to no intervention; it is an alternative to inadvertent intervention, which may be adverse.

The traditional American antipathy for intervention is often linked to a different point: that to impose U.S. or Western European institutions and procedures on developing countries is neither feasible nor desirable. Those who advocate stronger political development efforts usually are well aware of the need to adapt Western forms and to develop essentially new institutions in response to different national circumstances and political cultures. They do not have in mind carbon copies of U.S. or British institutions. But as noted earlier, many political development advocates do emphasize certain aspects, particularly equity and broadened political participation, more than other aspects, including national integration, administrative capacity, and development of civil liberties. These priorities may be quite appropriate in some of the developing countries. In others basic administrative competence and capacity to maintain civil peace, or national integration, or some other aspect of political development may take priority. Any direct or indirect promotion of political development should be based on a far more careful assessment than the U.S. Government now attempts of individual countries' political development trends, prospects, and priorities.

Assuming such analysis were available, what are the chances that foreign aid could really influence political development? No one really knows what might be accomplished, because no serious effort has yet been made. It is clear that the two major impediments are our own ignorance and host country sensitivity. Our ignorance argues for a cautious and experimental approach, rather than for bold departures. Diplomatic prudence points in the same direction. Regarding risk, however, it should be noted that political development activities do not have to be identified as such. Moreover, not all aspects of political development are particularly sensitive in every country. When U.S. goals coincide with the host government's and the topic is not extremely touchy, fairly open consultation and cooperation may be possible. For example, there may be mutual interest in strengthening local government institutions or promoting regional integration. Finally, if an objective is important, it is probably worth some risk. The United States has been increasingly willing to intervene in delicate economic decisions, such as devaluation, when it believes there is a reasonable chance of influencing host government action.

Nonetheless, doubts about the prudence, feasibility, and appropriateness of political development efforts continue to inhibit A.I.D.'s action in this realm. Does the Department of State have a stronger interest in political development? Some of the studies of particular developing countries written by members of the Department's Policy Planning Council have attempted systematic analyses of political development prospects. But most of the Department's political analysis centers on current events and problems. A time horizon longer than a year or 18 months is rare. Moreover, much Department analysis focuses on other countries' attitudes toward the United States and their positions on foreign policy issues of concern to the United States, rather than on attitudes and trends affecting their internal political development. There is some tendency to equate friendliness toward the United States and support for U.S. foreign policies with healthy political evolution. Even when analysis does focus on long-run problems of internal political development, the implications for concrete U.S. action are not worked out.

These tendencies are built into the system. Political officers are required to report information on the current situation and prospects for the immediate future. An Ambassador is expected to maintain cordial relations, to encourage understanding of U.S. international policies, and perhaps to have some impact on current problems while he is in a country. But no one assesses retrospectively the impact of the action or inaction of the U.S. Ambassador or Political Officer serving in that country five or ten years earlier.

Proposals for More Vigorous Political Development Efforts

Concern that inadequate attention is being given to the actual and potential impact of aid on long-run political evolution is not new to the foreign aid program. But in the last two years, self-examination within A.I.D. and Congressional criticism on this score has sharply intensified. In autumn 1964, A.I.D. Administrator David Bell, addressing an academic conference on political development held at the University of Pennsylvania, described development of democratic institutions and support for broadened political participation as important aspects of A.I.D.'s goals. He suggested that more vigorous and imaginative efforts might be needed.

During 1965 and early 1966, Representative Donald Fraser (Democrat, Minnesota), a thoughtful and continuing advocate of greater attention to political development, informally circulated in Washington a paper on the problem and the role he felt A.I.D. should play. Fraser defined political development in terms of "fostering, stimulating and guidance of fundamental social structures and behaviors that make effective self-government possible." He drew an analogy between current A.I.D. practice, as he saw it, of promoting economic growth and providing assistance against immediate security threats, and parents who see to their children's physical security and nutrition but fail to guide and support their emotional and social maturation. Fraser argued that one reason for neglect of the major foreign policy objective of political development was lack of a focal point within the U.S. Government where responsibility for and operational competence in political development was concentrated. He did not believe that the Department of State could take on this assignment; in his judgment, the Department's role, beyond the provision of broad policy guidelines, was to "deal with existing governments and provide reports and analysis." He concluded that the most appropriate existing agency to assume primary responsibility for political development was A.I.D.[4]

At about the same time a group of 25 Republican members of the House, led by Representative Bradford Morse (Republican, Massachusetts), were formulating a set of recommendations to improve the aid program. Two main themes underlay most of their recommendations: increased emphasis on administrative competence in the developing countries, and more stress on popular participation in and widely diffused benefits from development. The report urged that "no government-to-government aid should be extended to a country that shows no interest in holding popular elections, establishing broad suffrage, or creating a civil service based on merit. . ." or to governments where corruption and inefficiency blocked progress and were not being corrected.[5]

More recently, Vice-President Hubert H. Humphrey suggested, in a speech reportedly screened at both the White House and the State Department,[6] that "Our people and leaders [of the United

---

[4] *Congressional Record,* July 13, 1966, pp. 14765-14767.
[5] *Congressional Record,* March 15, 1966, p. 5601.
[6] *New York Times,* November 11, 1966.

States and the Latin American republics] should consider giving the same attention to political development that has been given in the past two decades to economic development." The Vice-President continued:

Economic and social development can help significantly to provide the basis for civic advancement, but it will not guarantee it. The past and prospective inadequacy of economic and social progress argues strongly for more conscious action to develop political systems that can enable rapidly changing societies to contain and manage explosive tensions.[7]

Much of this growing interest in political development crystallized in a new section in the Foreign Assistance Act of 1966. The House Foreign Affairs Committee report on the 1966 bill stated:

There is a close relationship between popular participation in the process of development and the effectiveness of this process. . . . Failure to engage all of the available human resources in the task of development not only acts as a brake on economic growth but also does little to cure the basic causes of social and political instability which pose a constant threat to the gains being achieved on economic fronts.[8]

Therefore, the Committee proposed and the House and Senate subsequently approved a new Title IX for the Act, entitled "Utilization of Democratic Institutions in Development." The Title reads:

In carrying out the programs authorized . . . emphasis shall be placed on assuring maximum participation in the task of development on the part of the people of the developing countries, through the encouragement of democratic private and local governmental institutions.

Congress also instructed the Executive Branch, in providing development loans and technical assistance in the future, to take into account ". . .the degree to which the recipient country is making progress toward respect for the rule of law, freedom of expression and of the press, and recognition of the importance of individual freedom, initiative, and private enterprise." [9]

Many of those advocating stronger political development efforts also urge more specific action bearing directly on politicians and political processes. Donald Fraser has proposed that A.I.D. should sponsor "a new institute to be termed a Center for Democratic Development to carry on those activities which the government finds

[7] Remarks of Vice-President Hubert H. Humphrey, Operation Amigo Dinner, Pan American Union, Washington, D.C., November 10, 1966.

[8] 89th Congress, 2d session, House Report No. 1651, June 23, 1966.

[9] Foreign Assistance Act of 1966, Sections 102(a)(1) and 103(a)(1), amending Sections 201(b) and 211 of the 1961 Act.

difficult to do directly." Representatives Fraser, Bradford Morse, and others have called for exchanges of North American and South American politicians in order to promote political development. The Republican group advocated, among other measures, that the assistance program give higher priority to training of social and political science teachers and preparation and distribution of texts on "theoretical and practical aspects of political science." [10] Morse and others have suggested offering assistance in establishing legislative reference services. Samuel P. Huntington of Harvard University has stressed the need for development of political institutions as the core of political development, and concluded that American policy should be directed to the creation within modernizing countries of "at least one strong non-Communist party." [11]

Proposals to assist and attempts to influence explicitly political institutions and groups may be labelled the "direct action approach." Most direct action proposals carry high diplomatic risks. The reaction in Chile and throughout Latin America to the Project Camelot should have reminded us, if reminders were necessary, of sensitivities in this realm. Camelot, after all, was to have been not an action program but Government-sponsored research into the causes of political stability and instability in Chile. Aside from the matter of prudence, the relevance or feasibility of some of the direct action proposals can be questioned.[12] However, there are undoubtedly some direct action programs that would be worthwhile. Normally private foundations or organizations are more appropriate sponsors for such programs than the U.S. Government or any of its agencies, as several of the advocates of direct action recognize.

There is much wider scope through indirect means for both private and governmental agencies to encourage national integration, equity, wide and responsible participation in decision making, and growing respect for civil liberties and democratic political processes. Indeed, although the indirect approach may appear slower, it is less risky, more flexible, and in the long run probably more powerful. Both political sensitivities and our limited understanding of political processes in the developing countries make it advisable to channel

[10] *Congressional Record,* March 15, 1966, p. 5601–5602.

[11] S. P. Huntington, "Political Development and Political Decay," *World Politics,* Vol. XVII, No. 3, April 1965, p. 429.

[12] For a fuller discussion of some of the proposals, see Robert Packenham, "Foreign Aid and Political Development," paper prepared for a symposium on "The Theory and Practice of Political Development," sponsored by the Brookings Institution and held at Airlie House in September 1966, pp. 23–25.

efforts to influence political development through the indirect and slow routes of building institutions (normally not explicitly political institutions), trying to influence the attitudes and sophistication of key groups, and encouraging the evolution of economic policies and structure, which in turn will support our long-term political objectives. Nonpolitical variables that affect the political system may provide more accessible and effective levers to encourage political development than do political variables per se.

It is tempting to list specific fields of activity that have been relatively neglected, and where considerably more could be attempted without serious risk. For example, A.I.D.'s contacts with the press and other information media have been limited, in part because it is assumed that the U.S. Information Agency has primary responsibility for this area. However, USIA efforts are largely directed to increasing understanding and knowledge of the United States and of U.S. positions on international issues. Much greater efforts could be undertaken, in cooperation with USIA, to build up the institutional basis for informed and responsible journalism and broadcasting on domestic as well as foreign issues in developing nations. A.I.D. could also do more to utilize its extensive contacts with business communities to encourage farsighted and informed participation in civic and political affairs. Legal education and municipal and local government have received little attention. Programs to expand and improve education could be more specifically and imaginatively designed to contribute to political development goals. For example, where ethnic or tribal divisions undermine national unity, higher teacher training institutions deliberately located and planned to draw students from several groups or tribes might be helpful.

But introduction of new activities or intensification of traditional efforts would merely extend the present, buckshot approach to promoting political development, without supplying the currently lacking analysis of individual country circumstances and the concentration on selected, clearly defined problems. Moreover, in a search for specific projects, more important problems and possibilities may be overlooked. For example, the overall effect of our assistance in many countries is to strengthen the central government. A.I.D. planners should be asking whether, under particular country circumstances, this effect is desirable. If it is not they can then consider what—if anything—can alter the impact. Such questions do not emerge from a project-oriented approach.

What is needed is the introduction of a serious political development dimension as an integral part of the programming process. This does not mean giving special priority to political development objectives, or necessarily including in each program some activities designed primarily to influence political development. It does call for explicit consideration of political development objectives and comparison of their priority with that of other goals, in the context of individual country circumstances and the nature of U.S. interests in the country. A political development dimension to aid programming also requires a continuing assessment of the ways in which the aid program as a whole, including aspects designed primarily to promote economic growth, may be affecting the aided country's long-run political evolution. At a minimum, such an assessment should reduce unanticipated adverse effects, and suggest ways to increase the political development by-products of primarily economic programs. Different country programs would vary in the extent to which they incorporated additional elements designed with political development objectives primarily in mind. The degree of emphasis on political development in individual programs would reflect the relative priority of political development goals, the extent to which they appear to conflict with or complement other goals such as rapid economic growth or short-run stability, and the likelihood that U.S. efforts to promote political development can be effective. Relying on the indirect approach, rather than attempting to influence specifically political institutions and processes, will reduce immediate diplomatic risk but will not automatically guarantee that actions best designed to promote political development will coincide with optimal economic policy. Under some circumstances long-run political gains may be worth some retardation of economic growth or some degree of short-run instability; in other cases economic growth or stability may be more important, or the possibility of effective U.S. action in the political development realm may be too remote to warrant detracting from other goals.

Filling in the "missing dimension of U.S. foreign policy" will require much better analysis of political development problems and prospects in individual countries than is now available. But current analytic resources within the U.S. Government are grossly incommensurate to the task. Identification and analysis of major problems in specific countries, and assessment of what, if anything, the United States can do about them cannot be handled on a part-time, informal basis or as a matter of individual interest. Yet A.I.D. has almost no staff responsible for conducting political development analysis. As of mid-1967, there is a three-man division in the worldwide Policy Planning Office assigned to political development questions. The Far East Bureau has a small political development unit, and one or two field missions have staff members with part-time responsibility for the area. In response to Congressional guidance as expressed in Title IX, A.I.D. will probably establish a few additional full-time positions for political development analysts. But it is not likely to build up a large staff in this realm.

While A.I.D. certainly should strengthen its capacity to assess political development problems, any significant and sustained U.S. effort will have to draw not only on new A.I.D. capacity but on the much more extensive potential analytic resources of the Department of State. The Department's Bureau of Intelligence and Research and the Embassy Political Sections abroad already have full-time responsibility for continuing analysis of countries' political situations and trends. Department analysis now focuses on leaders, parties, immediate pressures, and attitudes toward the United States rather than on problems of underlying political values and structure. To shift some part of the Department's and Embassies' attention to long-run problems of internal political evolution would require a substantial reorientation. Yet effective U.S. efforts to encourage political development are not and cannot be the sole responsibility of A.I.D. They will require the active collaboration of the entire U.S. foreign policy community.

Improved analysis of and efforts to promote political development will also require greatly improved communication between scholars and policy-makers. Much research is being conducted on political development. However, little of this research is brought to bear on problems of direct concern to A.I.D., or cast in terms that would assist a developing country to address its problems of political evolution. This situation contrasts with the quite active communication between A.I.D., the developing countries, and the research community with respect to economic development. It reflects much more limited and sporadic efforts on A.I.D.'s part to analyze problems of political development and to define the questions on which further research is needed. The lack of communication also suggests that most of those conducting research on political development have not attempted to spell out the policy implications of their work for the governments of the developing countries themselves or for U.S. government policies and programs. The lack of policy-oriented research and failure to try to apply the results of research are of course a vicious circle. Title IX's greatest contribution may turn out to be stimulation of efforts to bridge the gap between scholars and practitioners concerned with political development.

Just as we have had to learn that promoting self-sustaining growth in the less-developed world is a much more complex and long-run task than restoring war-torn Europe, so we have had to learn that the connection between economic progress and democratic political trends is much more tenuous in Asia, Africa, and Latin America than in Western Europe. We have barely begun to explore the extent and ways in which economic assistance, along with other instruments of foreign policy, may be used to promote political development. As analysis gets under way and specific lines of action are proposed, the principles derived from experience in using aid to encourage better economic policies may prove a useful guide. The most successful attempts to encourage economic reforms were based on extensive and detailed analysis of the specific problems to be addressed, often conducted over a period of several years. The reforms were also preceded by full and open consultation with the host government. In some cases the final impetus to reform depended partly on U.S. willingness to risk some diplomatic strain and some sacrifice of other goals. Although U.S. efforts to promote political development are likely to be less direct, the same broad principles are relevant.

Similarly, the factors constraining aid's effectiveness in encouraging economic reform will also limit the impact of political development efforts—concern that pressure for reform may jeopardize other high-priority U.S. objectives, inadequate understanding of the development process and the measures needed for particular kinds of progress, and political or administrative weakness on the part of the host government. In both the economic and political realms, the less secure and capable the regime, the poorer the prospects of adopting and implementing reforms. Those countries most in need of reform are least capable of responding to outside persuasion and support and are often the most sensitive and resistant to foreign influence. Aid cannot determine the course of a country's economic or political destiny. But in both realms, donors can stimulate fresh perspectives in countries open to suggestions and ideas, reinforce progressive forces, and reduce the internal costs and risks of reform. This is a marginal contribution, but it is often important and sometimes crucial.